D0119106

new
faux
finishes

H. John Johnsen

Sterling Publishing Co., Inc. | New York

Edited by Jeanette Green
Designed by Richard Oriolo
Photography by Robin Jay Lambert
Interior room designs by Susan A. Bell

LIBRARY OF CONGRESS CATALOGING-IN-PUBLICATION DATA AVAILABLE

1 2 3 4 5 6 7 8 9 10
Published by Sterling Publishing Company, Inc.
387 Park Avenue South, New York, N.Y. 10016
© 2001 by H. John Johnsen
Distributed in Canada by Sterling Publishing
c/o Canadian Manda Group, One Atlantic Avenue, Suite 105
Toronto, Ontario, Canada M6K 3E7
Distributed in Great Britain and Europe by Cassell PLC
Wellington House, 125 Strand, London WC2R 0BB, England
Distributed in Australia by Capricorn Link (Australia) Pty Ltd.
P.O. Box 704, Windsor, NSW 2756 Australia
Printed in China
All rights reserved

ISBN 0-8069-4461-7

contents

innovative faux finishes 77

faux finishes for wood molding 109

For my parents, who recognized my talent at a young age and put me on the right path

For Ilene Siegalovski, who helped me write this book

And for Jean for her perseverance and continued support

# introduction

d **id you ever** go into a house and see a beautiful faux finish on the walls and think, "Why can't I do that in my home?" Well, what stopped you? You probably thought the steps involved were too complex and time-consuming. Or, since you aren't a professional, it just wasn't possible to do it yourself. Guess again!

This book helps demonstrate that both assumptions are wrong. You can achieve faux finishes inexpensively and with few tools, many of which you may already own. All you need to do is follow a few simple directions. How hard can that be?

Over the last decade, faux finishes have become more and more popular. These versatile finishes add style, texture, and individuality to your home at little cost. Don't let any nervousness stop you. Remember that you found this book because you want to decorate your home with faux finishes. You'll be glad you did; you can add a lifetime of beauty to all the rooms in your house. Just try some of these techniques, and if you're not satisfied, you can always paint over the finish and begin again.

Just take a few minutes to learn how to apply the finish you choose, and you'll be surprised at the reward. Most of these techniques are fun and allow you to express your own creativity. Who knows, soon you may develop a faux finish of your own! So, choose a finish you'd like to try and begin.

the **color** palette

choosing the
perfect color

Colors...there are thousands of them! Or so it seems. Choosing colors today just seems difficult. You can choose yellow, green, plum, or hundreds of other colors that are out there. We'll show you a few ways to make choosing colors more fun and much easier.

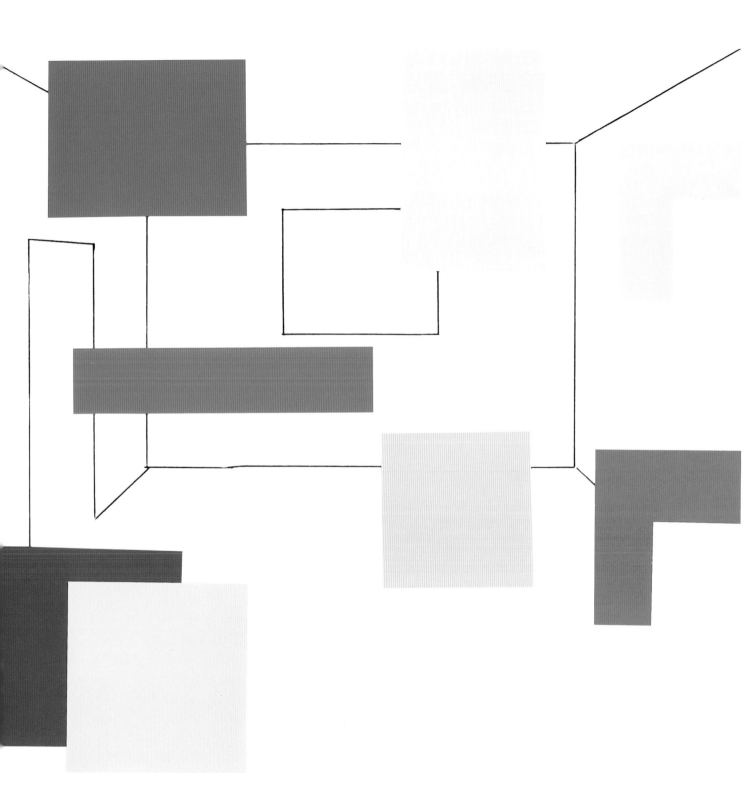

One is the favorite color or object plan. Do you already have a favorite color? If so, then look at different shades of that color. Compare the colors to the rest of the objects in the room you want to paint.

O.K. If you don't have a favorite color, how about looking at a favorite object in the room? It could be a vase, rug, or piece of furniture. Does this object have to stay in the room no matter what? Then work the color scheme around it. How? Find the predominant colors in the item. Now find shades or complementary colors that will work with that object.

If you have no favorite color or object, you're free to choose any color scheme that strikes your fancy. If you love all colors, there's a way to cut through this dilemma, too. We'll let you in on a secret that decorators and interior designers use when choosing their colors: architectural coloring.

Architectural coloring is a simple technique. If you use architectural coloring, you can forget about picking out a color right now. More confused? You thought this chapter would help you choose paint colors...it will, but not just yet. First, carefully look at the room(s) you want to paint. Then we'll guide you through the next step in color selection.

transforming a room with color

Architectural coloring can transform a room. How? First ask yourself a few questions. Is the room too small or too large? Is the ceiling too high or too low? Is the room too cold- or hot-looking (does it get too much sun or too little)? Are there any predominant colors in the room? After you've answered these questions or others that you may ask yourself, you'll be able to begin making successful color choices.

Of course, you're probably wondering, "How can answering these questions help me choose paint colors?" Answering these questions will help provide a direction for the colors that work best for the room you decorate. Here are basic things to consider:

Is the room small? To make the room appear larger, use one light color.

Is the room large? To make the room look smaller, use darker, deeper, and bolder colors.

Does the room have a low ceiling? To raise the ceiling, use white or light pastel colors.

Does the room have a high ceiling? To lower the ceiling, use warm or dark colors.

Does the room seem "cold"? To warm a cold-looking room, paint the walls yellow and the ceiling off-white.

Does the room seem "warm"? To cool a warm-looking room, use cool colors on the walls and white on the ceiling.

Is the hallway too long and narrow? To shorten or widen a long or narrow hall, use contrasting colors on opposite walls.

learning color terms

Painters, artists, and designers use special terms for their tools, materials, and concepts, and for describing what they do. Understanding color the way a painter or designer does may help you make informed color decisions.

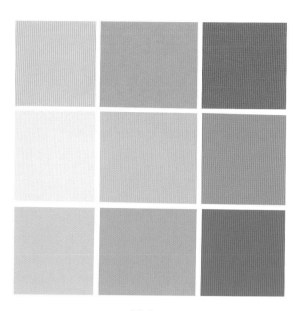

Value
the lightness to darkness of a color

Hue
the gradation of a color

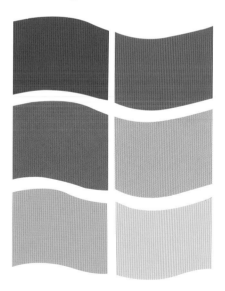

Shade
adding black to any color
Tint
adding white to create a lighter color

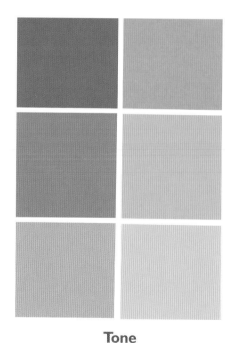

Tone
adding a touch of color opposite the color wheel; for example, to tone down pink (which is red), add green

Intensity

the brightness, dullness, or lack of

gray in a color

Monochromatic

one color and variations of that color

Analogous

colors immediately next to each

other on the color wheel

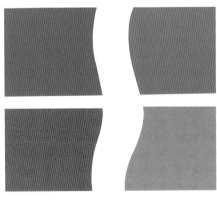

**Complementary or
Contrasting**

colors directly across from each

other on the color wheel

Triad Harmony

three color hues that may be used as a

basis for a color scheme; determined by

placing a triangle over a color wheel so

that the corners point to each color

what are color groups?

Simply stated, color groups will help you determine the visual temperature of a room. How does that work? Well, colors are classified into three groups: primary (warm), secondary (cool), and neutral.

Neutral

white, off-white, light brown, medium brown, dark
brown, light gray, medium gray, dark gray, black,
gold, and metallic chrome

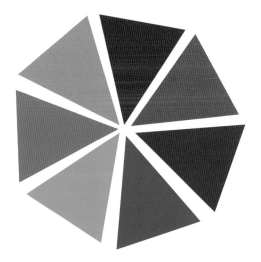

Cool

green, blue-green, blue, blue-purple,
purple, red-purple, and teal

Warm

red, red-orange, orange, yellow-orange, yellow, yellow-green,
warm beige, and peach

choosing the best paint finish

What's the best paint finish for your rooms? Do you want to buy flat, gloss, semigloss, or eggshell or satin? This question usually comes up when you are ordering paint. Sometimes choosing the finish seems as difficult as choosing the color. But don't let the many choices in paint finishes frustrate you. It'll become so easy that you'll quickly realize what you want. The first thing to consider is the use of the room.

A child's room requires paint that's impervious to everything. A paint that's impervious to all injuries is not yet available, but you could use a gloss or semigloss finish. This kind of paint allows easy cleanup of crayon, markers (some but unfortunately not all), and even scuff marks from shoes or other miscellaneous items. You won't be able to protect the walls from dents or dings or unknown objects that might be glued on them.

In the kitchen you could use semigloss. A semigloss finish makes cleaning any grease or spills that may hit the wall just a little easier. Use soap and water.

For the family room—in a house with young children—you can use semigloss or eggshell. Eggshell is similar to satin. Don't get confused now! Eggshell and satin clean up well, but they have less sheen (shine) than gloss and semigloss.

Here are the finishes and their advantages and disadvantages. Remember to take into account how the room is being used when choosing the finish. This will help you avoid repainting.

paint finishes

Gloss highly light-reflective, cleans up well, shows every flaw
Semigloss less reflective than gloss finish, cleans up very well, shows flaws
Satin or Eggshell absorbs light, cleans up well, shows fewer flaws
Flat no light reflection, cleans up poorly, hides flaws

the psychology of colors

Colors evoke many reactions. I remember walking into a room and feeling hungry; however, my friends wanted to leave immediately. Colors can have a profound effect on people. Because of the emotions colors stir up, two or more people may find it difficult to agree on color choices.

Let's consider various colors and how they affect our moods. Yellow may make you feel warm while it may stimulate someone else's memory. Oddly enough, yellow is the least often chosen home-decorating color. Some studies have suggested that calm, less energetic people seem more comfortable with cool colors, and that active, outgoing types prefer contrasting colors. Which type are you? What are your natural preferences? You may be surprised!

Red highly emotional; stimulates appetite, commands attention, raises blood pressure, conjures up love and lust

Pink sweetness; short-term calming effect

Yellow sunshine, warmth, feeling of newness; stimulates memory; many people avoid this color for home decorating

Orange vigor, boldness, ambition; brings happiness, stimulates thirst

Green relaxation, springtime, outdoors, fresh scents; the most restful color

Blue trust, ("true blue"); cool like water; if deep hue, communication; the most popular color

Purple royalty and religion; suppresses appetite

The Lime Butterfly

Black elegance, dignity, power, mystery, magic, as well as surrender

White cleanliness, purity, youthfulness

Brown warmth, comfort; associated with foods—breads, cereals, and more

Gray discipline, intelligence

lighting & colors

Does lighting affect colors? It sure does! Light is another example of how colors are affected. Look at a color (any one) inside your home. Now take it outside. Wow! There is a difference...right? Why does this happen? Well, it is because the light absorbs or reflects the color. Don't worry, I am not going to make this a science lesson.

To put it in simple terms, colors look different in the daylight or by various types of bulb. Standard lightbulbs (incandescent) tend to tone down colors, while tube (fluorescent) lights brighten colors. On the other hand, outside light can warm colors. OK, now you're confused. Don't be, I've included some examples of how light affects certain colors to make it easier to understand.

Incandescent light *(lightbulb)* enhances yellow and orange, gives red an orange tint, dulls blue and violet.

Fluorescent light *(tube)* invigorates green, blue, and violet hues; washes out red, yellow, and orange.

Natural light *(outside or synthetic combination of bulb & tube)* warms red, tones down yellow, brightens blue, and darkens green.

Keep in mind that you need to look at the color swatches in both day and night lighting before painting. My suggestion would be to live with the color swatches for a few days. Color perceptions change, and after a couple days you may see the colors differently.

bringing colors together

Colors have different effects when placed next to each other. When red is placed against white, the red appears brighter and lighter. But that same red against black looks dull. What happens when the red is next to green? The red seems stronger and brighter. Of course those "vibrating" colors can be used to create an exciting and colorful room. How about a white couch with red-and-green throw pillows? Pretty exciting, right?!

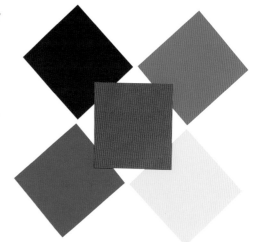

Side-by-Side Colors
Red next to blue Red takes on a yellowed tint.
Red next to green Red appears brighter and stronger.
Red next to yellow Red seems bluer.
Red next to black Red appears duller.
Red next to white Red seems brighter and lighter.

What happens when a light color is against a different but darker color? Well, it may seem obvious; the light color appears lighter. The darker one, of course, appears darker! This is called, in artist's jargon, "contrast of tone." Remember that old saying, "opposites attract"? This holds true even with colors. Remember the color wheel? Colors opposite each other on the color wheel tend to strengthen each other when used together. Here's what I mean...

Red appears redder with green.
Yellow seems sharper with purple.
Blue becomes bluer with orange.

You've learned all you need to know to be confident in your color decisions; now you can choose your paint colors from among the available paint samples, cards, and chips that manufacturers provide. Remember to have fun. This is not work—it's a way to relax and express your creativity.

styles, colors & faux finishes

Have you gotten tired of looking at the same old rooms? We all do, but the rooms in your house or apartment probably don't have to be redecorated—just repainted! A fresh coat of paint can give each room a new and different look! And with a faux finish your rooms take on a beauty unsurpassed by just a standard coat of flat paint.

In decorating, a sure way of creating a pleasing color balance is to keep most of the room in the shades of one color. Then balance this color with a harmonious second color. How about using one color and a few accent colors, such as white with blue or green with white?

Traditionalists usually advise us to use the darkest colors on the floors, medium colors on the walls, and the lightest colors on the ceiling. I say do what pleases you. It's your room. Forget about tradition...and these and other rules.

However, you may have a common dilemma. Your room is already decorated in a period or style. So then what do you do? Faux-finish the walls, of course! Now you could ask whether certain faux finishes would complement your particular style. Of course. Make a list of the various design styles with the finishes that you feel would fit your furniture and the character of your room best. When you look at the samples here, decide for yourself which style(s) you prefer. Then you can turn to the chapter that teaches you how step by step to apply paint using each technique.

eclectic *mixed styles and colors*
faux finish: depending on the predominant style, most finishes

english country *warm, slightly faded colors*
faux finish: paper pressing or stippling with light colors

french country *light, pastel colors*
faux finish: paper pressing or Old World walls

american country *bright, warm colors*
faux finish: sponging, ragging, or faux wallpaper

scandinavian country *cool, crisp colors with blue and white checks*
faux finish: sponging or ragging

arts & crafts *greens, blues, browns, copper, and bronze*
faux finish: color layering or brush swirling

american southwest *bright colors with black*
faux finish: brush swirling or color layering

regency or federal *strong yellow, emerald with crimson, deep pinks, and deep blues*
faux finish: strié or striping

georgian *scarlet red, emerald green with black and gold*
faux finish: strié or striping

victorian *deep, rich colors like deep blue, brown, olive green, and magenta*
faux finish: faux wallpaper or strié

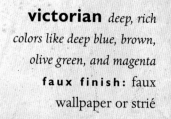

modern *ultramarine, lilac, various reds with black and silver accents*
faux finish: color layering, strié, or striping

neoclassical *reds, yellows, lilac, and green*
faux finish: color layering, Old World, or strié

Please keep in mind that this list of traditional styles is just a guide to prompt you to discover the style that suits your taste. Be creative and have fun. Choose the finish that fits your particular lifestyle. Don't forget to check the fabrics and furnishings in the room to make sure that the wall colors you've chosen will harmonize with them. View the color swatches and paint chips in the room in both daylight and evening lighting. You'll be surprised at how the colors can change in different light. Try it next to the curtains and windows. Then move the color swatch or paint chip around the room to see how the color expresses itself in shadows and near other pieces of furniture. You'll be amazed at how different the color appears in these different locations.

the ceiling...a forgotten area

OK, you're probably thinking, "Who looks up?" Actually, most people do look up when entering a room. How could you enter a room and not see the ceiling? So, what can you do? Many things can make the ceiling more attractive.

How about a faux finish, moldings, designs, or stencils? Few people bother to paint faux finishes on ceilings; imagine how unique such a finish would make your home. Moldings can create the illusion of a higher or lower ceiling. If you attach moldings to the wall 1 or 2 inches below the ceiling edge, you can make the ceiling appear lower. If you attach moldings about 1 inch in from the corner, the ceiling will appear higher.

Painting a sky on a ceiling can be great fun and perfect for a kid's room. A painted ceiling can be an extension of the walls' faux design, without a definite border. Stenciling offers many design possibilities. You can buy ready-made stencils or make your own (refer to the "Faux Wallpaper" technique on p. 100-102). It's often more rewarding to make your own stencils. Take your time to plan the new look and task carefully. Don't neglect the ceiling—you wouldn't go out without combing your hair.

preparing your
work area

in your work area the motto "Be Prepared" is most important. I have listed tools and materials that will help you accomplish your tasks efficiently and safely. I also have included a checklist that I use when working on projects for clients. This helps me be prepared for any situation that may arise. Don't forget the most important list: safety equipment that should always be incorporated in your work area. Each and every project in this book will require most if not all of the items in this safety-first list. These tools are standard and readily available at most paint and hardware stores.

your health & safety

Don't disregard the cautions here. Safety must always be your first concern. While you paint, you want to stay healthy, avoid accidents, and protect all members of the household. Consider the needs of aging parents, spouses, or roommates; children; pets; and people in ill health or who may use a wheelchair, for instance. Handle paint products with care and avoid breathing in the fumes.

Worktable (for mixing paints)

Drop cloths (to cover floor and furniture)

Stepladder (in excellent condition)

Trash container and garbage bags

Paint scraper(s)

Paint-stirring sticks

Sandpaper & sanding block

Empty bucket(s) for mixing paints

Tack cloth (for cleaning sanding dust)

Oak tag or Bristol board (to test mixed colors)

Spackling compound

Absorbent rags and paper towels

Primer paint

Paintbrushes

Paint strainers

Rubber bands

Empty paint cans and lids

Paint roller, tray, extension pole

Safety-First Supplies

Rubber gloves (don't use latex if you're allergic)

Paint-cleaning solvent (water or paint thinner)

Respirator (face mask for solvent fumes)

Portable fan

Ventilation: Always keep the area you're working in well ventilated when using alkyd (oil), paint thinners, and solvents. Open a window and use a fan. This will keep the air circulating and allow fresh air into the room. You don't want the fumes to build up. Many paint and other fumes are flammable. Avoid using gas stoves, space heaters, and candles. Don't smoke in the area. Take the time to carefully read all the directions on the cans before using the products. Isn't being safe worth a few minutes of reading? Of course, you'll want to choose a week when they're not putting new asphalt on the street outside your house or apartment building. You don't want to combine fumes or track tar indoors.

No Smoking: Remember that paint fumes, especially alkyd (oil), paint thinners, and solvents, are flammable. Absolutely no smoking in or near the area being painted! You or people you love

could suffer serious burns. Even if you aren't using alkyd or oil paints, you could get ashes in the paint. If you're a confirmed smoker, take a break, go outside, and stand well away from the building.

Gloves: Always wear rubber gloves when using these products and while performing the techniques in this book. Use gloves both to make cleanup easier and to protect your skin from any product chemicals.

Respirator: These face masks come in a few varieties. The simplest is the paper mask that protects you from breathing in dust, wood shavings, and paint chips. The single-filter face mask is used for solvents, such as paint thinner. The double-filter face mask can be used for heavy-duty projects, such as furniture stripping.

Ladders: Even if you are working just a few feet off the ground, keep that ladder stable. Make sure that it is always fully opened or secured while leaning against a wall. A fall of only a few feet (or a meter) could be very painful.

Lighting: To view your work properly, the area should be well lit. You couldn't work in the dark, and working in a dimly lit room would be just as foolish.

Traffic: If your home has a lot of traffic (and whose doesn't?), keep all your equipment contained in one area. You don't want anyone tripping on a paint can or drop cloth. This could happen in broad daylight to able-bodied people or athletes as well as the usual household variety of clumsy folk. Also consider the work area during your down time. You don't want someone halted on a midnight tour of the refrigerator knocking over the solvent or indeed adding it to a Dagwood sandwich instead of mayonnaise. Your teenage ballerina may accidentally create a *Swan Lake* impression on your newly finished wall. You may find aboriginal handprints on your in-progress art-deco floor. Think of the possibilities. While these thoughts may be amusing, the aggravation, injury, and repair will not be. Provide a clear corridor around the work so that everyone is happy and safe. Find ways to keep children and pets and everyone else, if you can, out of the room until the paint dries and the air is again clean and fresh.

Children: Always keep children away from all paints, solvents, ladders, rags, and equipment. These can be potentially harmful. If possible, keep the room closed but windows open (even a crack will help) when you are not working. Paint and other fumes can harm children, who are smaller than adults and have immature lungs, much more easily and quickly.

The Elderly & People with Special Health Needs: If someone with asthma, emphysema, allergies, or another health consideration lives in the household, please consult a physician. You can also contact the paint, glaze, or solvent manufacturer to ask about any concerns you might have about their products. Some people are allergic to latex, whether in drying paints or rubber gloves. Remember that fresh air is always better for someone with heart disease, just as it is better for the healthy. Don't take chances. Be smart and enjoy your project!

Pets: Curious cats and companionable dogs can make havoc of a work area and find themselves in trouble. Don't give them a chance to check out your paintbrushes, half-empty buckets, and drop cloths. Allow the finished room to air out a few days before you allow any pet(s) to sniff the walls. Don't test air quality with your canary. Remember that pets are much smaller than we are; just a little toxin can go a long way.

preparing the surface

Prep...prep...prep. The success of faux finishing begins with proper surface preparation. I know this is the boring, no-fun part. However, if you want a beautiful finish, the surface must be clean and free of imperfections. About 25% of the time that you'll need for your project will be devoted to the wearying art of preparation. In the end, that's not really a lot of time if you want professional results. I know you want to paint, and you will, but preparation must come first. Check the walls. Do you see any cracks or holes? Repair these before painting. Holes or cracks will destroy the finish you hope to accomplish. Remember this is a vital stage and will affect the durability and appearance of the finish.

Flaking Paint

Flaking paint should be removed with a paint scraper. You can smooth the remaining sharp edges by sanding with 120–220-grit nonfilling sandpaper. Sand the wall, floor, or ceiling until the edges are even with the surrounding surface. Now slide your fingertips over the sanded area. Does it feel smooth compared to the rest of the wall? If it does, then you can wipe the wall down. Don't just wipe the sanded spot. There will be sanding dust on the surrounding areas, so you'll have to wipe down the whole wall with a damp cloth. Be vigilant when cleaning the moldings above doors and windows. These always catch dust and debris. Once the surface is wiped down, you'll be ready to proceed.

Spackling Holes & Cracks

Every home has cracks or holes in its walls. Cracks usually result from settling foundations, and holes come from various objects once attached to the walls. Small holes can be filled with spackling compound. Shallow cracks may be difficult to fill, so you may have to open the crack slightly with a sharp knife. This will help the Spackle stay in place. Before filling the

Open crack slightly with a utility knife.

Clean out debris.

Spackle with thin coats.

opened crack, clean out any debris and wipe the crack and area around it with a damp cloth.

When it's time to spackle, apply Spackle with a spackling knife using thin coats. Thick coats tend to crack as they dry. Allow each coat to dry before applying the next coat. Your patience will be rewarded with a beautiful finish. Just press the Spackle into the opening. Let it dry and then sand.

Use a sanding block, a piece of wood about 3 x 3 inches (7.5 x 7.5 cm) with sandpaper attached. You can easily make your own. If you don't have any wood scraps, check with a neighbor. Make sure the sanding block will fit into the palm of your hand. Using this block will keep the surface level. Just using your hand and a sheet of sandpaper could cause ripples.

As you are sanding, feel the repaired area. Does it feel even with the rest of the wall? If not, you can apply a second coat. Keep adding thin layers until the repaired area is level with the surrounding surface. Remember: Allow each coat to dry thoroughly before applying the next.

Large holes or cracks will require additional work. If your walls require extensive repairs, consider hiring a professional. You could, however, tackle this time-consuming job yourself. It's worth the effort. Cover the holes or cracks with spackling tape or crack-repair screen (available at most hardware stores). Then fill the repair with spackling compound. Again apply thin layers and allow plenty of time for each layer to dry. Lightly sand the repaired area and run your hand over it to feel whether it is level with the rest of the wall. If necessary, repeat the process until the repaired spot is level.

After the repaired area has been sanded smooth, wipe it with a damp cloth to remove any residual sanding dust. Then wipe the whole wall and floor molding.

Priming

The next step, priming the repaired area, is very important. If you don't properly prime the repair, it will show through your work. Apply a thin layer of primer over the repaired area several times. I know you'd prefer to just begin painting, but you need to wait until this work is done. Look at it this way: The wall already has several coats of paint, and the repaired area has no coats of paint. To equalize them, you need to build up the paint on the repaired surface. Brush on a thin coat of paint and feather out the area. You "feather" by brushing over the edges of the new paint with the same brush, softening them, before the paint dries. Allow each coat to dry thoroughly before applying the next coat of paint.

Cleaning the Surface

Unless your home is brand new, your walls could use a simple cleaning. Even walls in perfect condition may need to be cleaned. This may not be easy, but it's well worth the effort. I know; I learned the hard way. How? Run your finger over the tops of molding in any room. Surprised? Well, the dirt on your finger can be dragged through paint by a brush or roller, leaving a less-than-perfect finish. Before cleaning the walls, cover the floor and furniture with drop cloths. That way you'll be prepared when you begin to paint. Wipe the walls with a slightly damp cloth.

Washing Walls

Use a damp cloth. When cleaning walls, always start from the top and work down. This will help avoid dirty-water streaks. The final rinse should be clean water. Allow the wall to dry. The drying process is critical; so let the surface dry for a day or two. Remember...patience. Painting before the surface is completely dry will trap moisture and eventually cause your work to mildew or flake. I'm sure you don't want a beautiful finish to mildew or flake—especially not after all this work.

Wax or mildew may also create plaque on walls. Here's how you can remove them.

Wax Removal: Wax in any form, including crayon, can be removed easily with benzene (naphtha). Keep the area well ventilated. Wash the cleaned area with household cleaner and rinse thoroughly with clean water to remove any remaining residue.

Mildew Removal: Mildew is caused by a combination of too much moisture and lack of sunlight. You must remove it before priming. First, use household bleach to remove as much of the mildew as possible. Remember to use protective gloves and a face mask to avoid the fumes. Let the surface dry thoroughly. Now, apply a coat of mildew-preventative paint (available at your local hardware or paint store), and let it dry according to the manufacturer's recommendations.

Kitchens

Kitchens are a different subject. Years of smoke, grease, and dirt accumulate and leave a film. Use a household detergent to clean the kitchen walls and ceiling. This is a necessary step in creating a great-looking kitchen. If your walls are pretty clean, you can eliminate the rest of this section.

When using cleaning solutions, always be sure to have proper ventilation. Open windows and use fans. Read all the warnings on the can. If necessary, wear a respirator.

Removing Wallpaper

You should always remove wallpaper, even if the wall underneath is not in the best condition. Painting over wallpaper could cause it to peel off and ruin your finish.

This is a tedious project and not one of my favorites. But it will make a world of difference if you no longer want the wallpaper. I know. After removing pinkish—yes, pinkish—wallpaper, the room was totally transformed. And isn't that what you'd like to accomplish?

Before beginning, cover the floors and furniture with drop cloths. Next, carefully cut very shallow slits in the paper. You can use a utility knife or a straight-edge razor in a protective handle. Cut deep enough into the paper without cutting into the wall. Use a light touch. If you cut too deeply you will have cut marks in the wall. The slits allow the stripper to work faster by soaking into the glue layer. Otherwise it would just sit on the surface and dry, and that wouldn't help.

Soak the paper with a wallpaper stripper using a brush or sponge. Some papers will come off easily; others will take more time to remove. You may have to apply the stripper several times, but always keep the paper wet. After all the paper is removed, wash the walls down using a mild detergent. This will remove any wallpaper-paste residue. Let the walls dry for a few days. Then apply a base coat of primer to give the top coat a sound base.

Masking Paint Projects with Tape

Many tapes are on the market. The type of tape you choose depends on the project, the type of surface you are painting, and the length of time the tape will be on the wall. I prefer the blue tape. Why? It can stay on the walls for a few days and be removed without destroying the surface. But you will need tape only if your project requires it. Taping helps to prevent paint seepage and keeps a clean and sharp edge. Tapes are available in a wide range of sizes and widths. The "Tapes for Paint Projects" descriptions on p. 40 will help you determine the right tape for your particular project.

When applying tape, press down on its edge only. If you put pressure on the middle of the tape, that may make it more difficult to remove. The secret to creating a sharp edge for painting is to burnish the edges (rub the edges securely); otherwise paint seepage could occur. When taping moldings, place the tape as close as you can to where the molding meets the wall.

Remove the tape as soon as possible after you've completed your project. Remember this little trick to removing the tape: Pull the tape away from the surface at a 45-degree angle using a moderate speed. If you remove the tape fast, it could tear into strips or maybe take some of the finish away with it. If you remove it too slowly, it could leave adhesive residue. Don't worry if that happens, because any residue can be removed with acetone or paint thinner on a Q-tip. Be sure to test the thinner on a paint swatch to ensure it won't damage the surface.

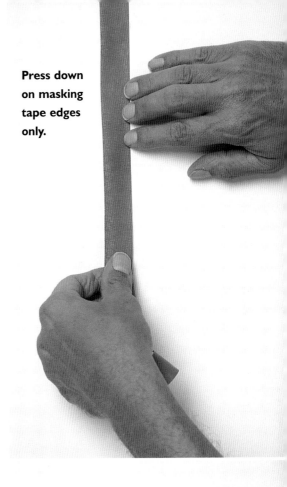

Press down on masking tape edges only.

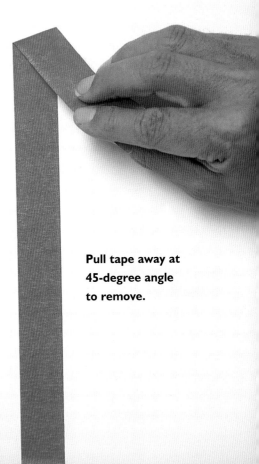

Pull tape away at 45-degree angle to remove.

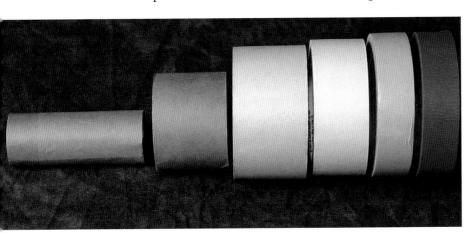

Painter's Tape: This craft-paper tape comes in 2- to 6-inch widths. It is lightly gummed on half of its width. This tape is stiff and cannot be used on curves. It also doesn't stick to itself, so you cannot overlap it. Also the tape will not adhere to a wall surface for long periods of time. It is, however, good for straight-edge lines or specific width spaces.

Masking Tape: This is available in $1/8$- to 4-inch widths. The tack (stick) quality varies widely from manufacturer to manufacturer. Test this tape on an inconspicuous area to check for any damage or residual glue when it is removed. Masking tape should not be left on for more than 24 hours since it could damage the surface. However, it is excellent for quick projects. A cheap masking tape may shred into multiple pieces when applied or removed.

Extended-Release (Blue) Tape: This blue tape, preferred by most decorative painters, comes in 1- to 2-inch widths. This tape can be left in place for longer periods of time (several days) without damaging the surface or leaving any residue. It costs more than masking tape, but I feel the ease of application and the easy cleanup are worth the extra cost.

Chart Tape: These come in $1/64$- to 1-inch widths. Chart tapes, available in art-supply stores, can be used for special effects. No projects in this book require this type of tape, but you may create a use.

Primers

Using a primer is an important part of your project. If your walls are old or if you're not sure that the existing finish is suitable, because of repairs or dirt from age, then prime.

This primer coat will give you a fresh palette to work on. Yes...think of the walls as a palette or canvas. Since you are the artist, you want it to be perfect, or at least as close to perfect as you can manage. The primer will seal the surface and make it less porous. This helps to ensure equal absorption of the top-coat layers, so you will need fewer coats of paint to achieve the final base-coat color. The proper preparation can actually save you time and work later.

Although a wide variety of primers are available, we'll concentrate on the two most important types: water-based and oil-based. You can use water-based primers for latex (water-based) or oil (alkyd) paints, but oil-based primers are for oil paints only.

Each type of primer has advantages on different surfaces. Alkyd or oil-based go on more smoothly and seal better than latex, but oil-based primers need a solvent (paint thinner or turpentine) for cleanup. Latex or water-based paints dry much more quickly. As long as they remain wet, they can be cleaned up easily with just water. You can also wash out paintbrushes and rollers with water, if you clean them immediately. If you happen to forget and get sidetracked before cleaning the paintbrushes—and who hasn't—use denatured alcohol to clean the dried latex paint. Read the manufacturer's (use-of-this-product) label before using denatured alcohol. Water-based paints dry in just 1 to 2 hours. Oil-based paints require 12 to 24 hours.

If you tint the primer the same color as the top coat, you won't need as many top coats. Your local paint store can tint the primer. Yes, you can tint oil or latex primers, too. Just show the clerk the color you're using, and he will tint the primer accordingly.

Straining Paint

You won't have to strain paint unless you've discovered a can of your favorite color of paint that's a few years old. Strain the paint to make sure you don't encounter unnecessary lumps or dried paint flakes. Lumps or flakes, caused by exposure to air, may be inside the lid. A few lumps or flakes can ruin your painted finish. If you're not sure whether you have to strain, the simplest way to find out is to stir the paint. If you see any clumps, strain.

To strain the paint, find a new, empty gallon paint can. Now find some old pantyhose. No pantyhose? Try an old sheer curtain; you only need a small piece. Now loosely stretch the pantyhose or curtain over the top of the can. Do not stretch the material too tightly. Leave a dip in the middle of the material for the paint to pool. If the material is too tight, the paint will run over the sides of the can and make a mess. Secure the material with a rubber band. Now you're ready to strain.

Another way to strain paint is to use a commercial paper-cone strainer, available at any paint store. Pour the paint slowly to allow it time to drain into the can. Straining paint can be time-consuming, but the results are worth the extra effort.

Loosely stretch pantyhose over the top of the paint can.

Secure pantyhose with a rubber band.

faux media &
finishes

paint basics

et's consider base-coat paints, decorative paints, glazes, and solvents. Remember that the two main types of paint are latex and oil. Each has its own advantages and disadvantages. Which kind you use depends on personal preference as well as drying time, workability, and cleanup. High humidity causes paint to dry much more slowly than normal.

water-based or latex paints

Water-based or latex paints come in a wide range of colors and tints. You can color the chosen paint to your exact specifications. These paints are odorless and dry quickly. Once dry, they are tough and water-resistant. It's important to clean brushes and paint drips with water immediately. You can correct any mistakes by wiping with a damp cloth before the paint dries. Undiluted latex paint has great covering ability. Diluted with water, the paint can appear similar to watercolors.

oil-based or alkyd paints

Oil-based or alkyd paints come in a limited choice of colors. They take from 12 to 24 hours to dry completely and give off strong fumes. Clean paint drips and brushes with paint thinner. Remember that most thinners for alkyd paints are flammable. Alkyd paints do, however, spread more easily and more smoothly than latex paints.

CAUTION Thinners for alkyd paints are flammable.

paints for decorative techniques

The next group of paints is for decorative techniques. These paints are generally not used as base coats because of their high cost.

acrylic paints

Acrylic paints are water-based. They come in a wide range of colors from a variety of manufacturers and are available at arts-and-crafts stores. Acrylics are highly regarded for their quality and durability. Although not inexpensive, they have the advantages of superior color, quick drying, durability, flexibility, and resistance to sunlight. Acrylics come in tubes, jars, and economy containers. They dry to a matte finish. These are used for tinting base coats, painting murals, and faux finishing.

If you'll be using a lot of the same color (say a lot of green), stay with one manufacturer. Why? Colors vary with different manufacturers. For instance, a light green from one manufacturer may look like a medium green from another manufacturer.

Here's a note of interest: Acrylic paints will not adhere to oil-based paints without sanding and then priming with acrylic gesso.

egg tempera

Egg tempera has a pigment suspended in an egg-oil emulsion. It dries to a matte finish. The paint will not stand up well to dampness. It also dries brittle, which makes it unsuitable for flexible surfaces like canvas. Egg tempera takes a long time to dry, but once dry it is extremely durable.

casein

Casein is similar to watercolor. However, it has more white pigment than watercolor, which gives it greater opacity. Casein remains water-soluble when completely dry, so to protect it, you must cover it with a layer of clear shellac.

gouache

Gouache is widely regarded for its brilliant colors and soft matte finish. It is also water-soluble when completely dry, but can be made indelible if you mix it with acrylic medium. However, this mixing technique reduces its color potency and affects the special soft matte finish.

artist's oils

Artist's oils are excellent for their quality and durability. They are available in a wide range of colors from many manufacturers. Oils are easy to blend and dry to a semigloss, translucent sheen. Unfortunately, the high content of oil results in a much longer drying time. They may take days or even longer to dry. If you're in no rush (and you shouldn't be), using oils can be advantageous. I prefer acrylics (due to time constraints), but am amazed at the results you can achieve with oils. Artist's oils are very expensive and must be cleaned with paint thinner. Remember that at one time, oils were the only paints available for artists.

japan colors

Japan colors have a limited color range. However, the available colors are intense, and they have the more desired earth and darker colors. Japan colors come in cans and can be used as decorative finishes or to tint other paints. They dry within a few hours to a matte finish. Unfortunately, they are not as easy to find as other paints. Look in the specialty-paint section of paint stores and in arts-and-craft stores.

solvents & thinners

You may be wondering: What's the difference between solvents and thinners? I used to wonder myself. Actually, it's quite simple. Solvents become thinners when they reduce the viscosity (thickness) of paints. They are solvents when

CAUTION When using solvents and thinners, open windows, use fans, and wear a respirator and chemical-resistant gloves.

used for cleaning brushes and surfaces. Keep in mind: All solvents and thinners should be used with adequate ventilation and while you are wearing a chemical respirator and chemical-resistant gloves. Take my advice...it comes from experience.

Paint thinner is also known as mineral spirits. It is similar to turpentine but less toxic. It is used for cleaning oil-based, or alkyd, paint. Read the label for warnings or cautions.

Water is the appropriate solvent for water-based latex and acrylic paints while they are still wet.

Denatured alcohol removes dried latex, acrylic paints, and shellac. Read the label for warnings or cautions.

the base coat

Applying the base coat is as important as preparing the surface. Before you begin, make sure the room is as free of dust as possible. Also protect the floor and furniture with drop cloths. Of course, the most important thing is the paint. Do you have enough? Always make sure you have enough paint before you start painting. How do you know if you have enough? Well, the average gallon covers about 300 square feet. Measure the room you are painting. How?

Here are a couple simple formulas for estimating how much paint you'll need to use before buying paint.

Walls: Measure the room's perimeter (the distance around the room) times the height. This will give you the approximate square footage. Two coats are usually sufficient. When using a different trim color, subtract any doors (usually 21 square feet each) and windows (usually 15 square feet each).
Ceilings: Measure the room length and multiply it by the width to determine the approximate square footage. Use the same formula if you are painting the floor.

If you are going to use more than 2 gallons, buy the paint premixed in a 5-gallon container. But if you are buying only 2 or 3, you can mix the gallon cans together in a large container to ensure the same hue throughout the project. Mix the paint thoroughly using a large paint stick or electric-drill paint stirrer. (Always use an electric stirrer at a slow speed so you don't get paint all over.) Then carefully pour the mixed paint back into the original cans and seal tightly until needed.

painting techniques

brush painting

When you are using a brush, it's wise to slightly thin the paint instead of using it directly from the can. Thinning the paint ensures a smoother finish and a shorter drying time. You can add a small amount of solvent (paint thinner for alkyd or water for latex) a little at a time. Don't make it too thin or it will run and drip. Then test the paint on an inconspicuous corner for finish smoothness.

Before using a new paintbrush, tap it gently across your hand to remove any dust or loose bristles that might remain from when it was manufactured. Now you're ready to paint. Dip the brush with one-half to two-thirds of the bristles into the paint. Apply the paint at a slight angle. Use a moderate but even pressure. Hold the brush near the bristles for a firm grip. You can eliminate any brush strokes by very lightly touching the brush to the surface and re-brushing.

Immediately clean the paintbrush in the appropriate solvent when finished. Place the brush in a container wide enough for the brush and for your hands. Then twirl the brush between your hands to expel any excess liquid. The container will keep the solvent and paint from flying everywhere and making a mess. Finally, place the brush in its cardboard sleeve, or wrap it in newspaper to protect the bristles. A piece of tape will hold the newspaper closed until you are ready to use the brush again. Don't use a rubber band because it will squeeze the bristles out of shape.

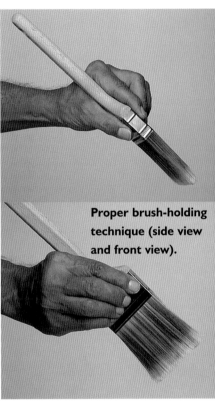

Proper brush-holding technique (side view and front view).

Twirl brush to expel excess liquid.

Tap brush to remove any loose bristles.

roller painting

For painting large surfaces I recommend a roller. Rollers make painting quicker and leave no brush marks. When purchasing rollers, keep in mind that you get what you pay for. For the best results, use the best tools. Surely you don't want pieces of roller felt or brush hairs to mar the finished surface.

Before rolling, cover the floor and furniture with drop cloths. Fill your roller tray so that half of the bottom is covered with paint. Dip the roller in the paint and roll a little of the excess back into the tray. Apply the paint in a crisscross direction. Work across the ceiling and down the walls.

design tip

If pieces of felt or brush bristles stick to the wet paint, you can remove them with a toothpick. Do not remove them with your fingertips because you will leave a mark.

Glazes are an important top coat for some finishes in this book. Glazes are translucent overlays of clear or tinted media that are manipulated over a dried base coat. Simply stated, paint the glaze on top of a dried painted surface. Glazes can add subtle or dramatic dimension and innovation to any room in your home. Don't be afraid to use them. They can transform a room into a showcase.

There are two types of glaze: latex and alkyd (oil). The alkyd dries much slower than latex and allows you more "workable" time. Both come premixed and are available at paint and arts-and-crafts stores.

Water-Based Glaze: Water-based glazes are thin and usually dry in only 20 minutes. This makes these glazes difficult to work with on large areas unless you have the help of an assistant. Unfortunately, we don't all have that pleasure. Instead, work on small areas (6 X 6 feet) due to the quick drying time. You can tint water-based glazes with latex paints, acrylic, casein, tempera, gouache, watercolor, and water-soluble powdered pigments. You can also make your own special color glaze. Clean the brushes and equipment with water.

Oil-Based Glaze: Oil-based glazes dry more slowly, in about 30 to 40 minutes. Therefore, they allow more working time than water-based glazes. Oil glaze is thick, so you will want to thin it with no more than 10% of paint thinner. Thin slowly, using a little at a time. A mixture that is too thin will run. This glaze can be tinted only with artist's oil colors, Japan colors, and universal tints. Mix thoroughly before applying to the surface. Clean paintbrushes and equipment with paint thinner.

Tinting a Glaze

If you are going to tint your own glaze, first determine the size of the area you want to cover. If you'll be using more than one can, it would be wise to combine them in one large container. This will keep the color uniform throughout the project. When mixing always add a small amount of color at a time and mix thoroughly. You don't want clumps of unmixed color to ruin your finish.

Test the results on a piece of primed oak tag or sheetrock. Allow the mixture to dry thoroughly to determine the proper color. Measurement containers can be measuring cups or plastic or paper cups.

design tip

Always keep a record of the type (manufacturer's name) and amount (gallon, quart, cup, etc.) of the glaze and the tinting agent (acrylic, oil, etc.) for each project. This is in case you need to repeat or repair any finishes. Also, write the project name and date with all pertinent information and record it on 3 × 5-inch cards or in a spiral binder. See "The Formula Notebook" on p. 55.

painting equipment

There are many different decorative painting tools, which range in price from a few to several hundred dollars. Don't worry; most finishes in this book don't require expensive paintbrushes. Most of the tools you'll need are inexpensive everyday objects. However, it won't hurt to know about other more specialized tools. You never know...these may spark painting creativity.

All craftspeople—carpenters, painters, and even chefs—have their own favorite tools. What all these people have in common is that they all know that the best-quality tools are the one that give superior results. If taken care of properly, great tools will last for years.

paintbrushes

An extensive range of paintbrushes is available through art stores and paint and hardware stores. Some are designed for painters and artists. Specialty brushes are for the decorative painter. Brush prices can range from a few dollars to several hundred dollars, depending on the type.

The two basic paintbrush types are synthetic and natural. Synthetic brushes are used for latex and natural brushes are for oil or alkyd paints. Remember that good-quality brushes are an important investment. Always clean the brushes thoroughly after each use and store them in tubes or containers to keep them clean and to protect the delicate bristles.

Cleaning Oil-Based Paintbrushes

Before cleaning the paintbrush, remove as much paint as possible. Do this by brushing the excess paint onto newspaper or cardboard. Find two containers of equal size to hold the brush. Fill both cans approximately one-third with paint thinner. Dip the paintbrush into the first container. Stir and swirl the brush around to remove the paint. Then place it into the second container and swirl it to remove any remaining paint.

Do not let the paintbrush sit in the solvent. This will cause the brush to lose its shape, and the bristles may begin to fall out. Find a bucket or empty

design tip

Remove any clogged paint by putting on a pair of rubber gloves and working the paint out of the bristles with your fingers.

design tip

When wrapping the paintbrushes with brown paper do not use a rubber band because it will squeeze the bristles out of shape.

If you are waiting for the paint to dry and don't want to clean the brush, just wrap the brush in plastic wrap to keep it from drying out.

container that's large enough to hold your hands as well as the paintbrush, or go outside. Hold the paintbrush by the handle between both hands and swirl out any excess thinner. Keep in mind that the swirling will throw the solvent on you and any surrounding area—that's why using a container is a better idea. Besides, do you want to clean up after cleaning up? Lay the brush out to dry and place it in its protective sleeve, or wrap it in brown paper and tape it closed.

Cleaning Water-Based Paintbrushes

You can use soap and warm water to rinse out brushes used in water-based paint. Work the soap into the bristles and up toward the ferrule to remove any deeply embedded paint. Do not bend the bristles; just work them in their natural direction with your fingertips. Rinse thoroughly with warm water to remove any remaining soap. Then spin or press out the water. Place the paintbrush in its protective sleeve or wrap it in brown paper to help keep its original shape. Use tape to hold the wrapping closed.

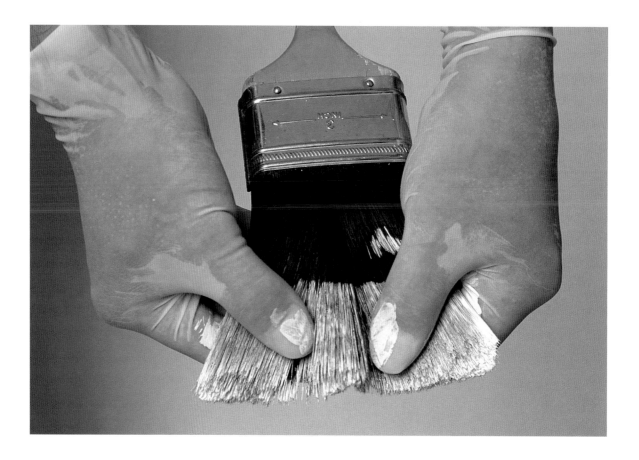

specialty brushes

In decorative painting a wide range of brushes can be used. Each brush is designed for a specific paint and/or technique. However, if use your creativity and experiment a little, you may find new uses for these brushes.

Because specialty brushes are made of different kinds of hairs, each may require slightly different handling. For instance, a badger hairbrush just needs its tips washed. If you attempt to wash the whole brush, the bristles fall out. Ask the brush salesperson or call the manufacturer if you are unsure about cleaning specialty brushes. These brushes may inspire new faux-finish designs.

Short-Haired Spalter for applying and smoothing oil glazes

Long-Haired Spalter for smoothing out oil glazes

Nylon Brush for detailing and mural painting with acrylic paints

White Bristle Brush for painting murals and pictures with artist's oil paints

Stencil Brush for stenciling with oils or acrylics

Badger-Hair Brush for smoothing out and blending glazes

Liner and Stripper Brushes for creating veins in marbling with acrylics

Toothbrush for spattering medium

Stipple Brush for removing glaze by pouncing, dragging, or turning; helpful for evening out glazes to create a translucent coat and for stippling paint onto a surface; available in various sizes

Wallpaper-Smoothing Brush for creating a soft or sharp strié when pulled through glaze

Flogger for creating strié texture or a porelike surface; its wide, long bristles are tapped on the surface

Toothed Spalter for creating specialty wood graining in oil glaze

Overgrainer for dragging and graining; nylon bristles are on one side and natural bristles on the other

Once you are familiar with the effects these brushes make, you will be able to devise your own creative finishes. Don't be afraid to experiment with these and other types of brush. How do you think I came up with some of these finishes? Experimentation!

specialty tools

You'll find these specialty tools at most craft and hobby stores. Be creative. If you look around, you'll discover how other household tools and materials can help create decorative-painting techniques.

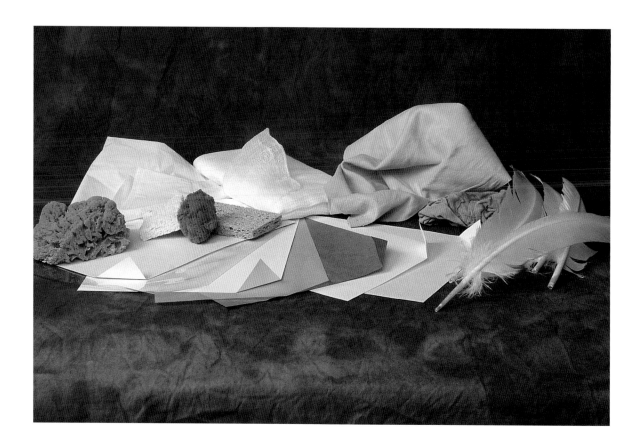

Sponges: Sponges can be natural (sea grass and wool) or synthetic (cellulose). Each will render a different type of finish and texture. Sponges must be wet with water and thoroughly wrung out before being used.

Plastic: Plastic in the form of bags, sheets of plastic wrap, or even an old shower curtain can create an interesting texture. Just press the plastic into a wet-paint or glaze surface and remove the plastic immediately. For various effects, plastic can also be manipulated with the hands and fingers.

Turkey Feathers: Turkey feathers can be used for marbling and graining. Place the feathers on the surface and flip them from side to side. Or pull the feather's tip through the medium to create veins.

Cheesecloth: Cheesecloth, a thin, gauzelike material, can be used for removing glazes. It can also add texture to decorative painting. Buy it at craft stores, hardware stores, or supermarkets. Fold the outside edges underneath to keep those loose threads from getting on your painted surface. For better absorbency, use a good grade of cheesecloth.

Paper: Any kind of paper can be a versatile and fun tool to use on decorative surfaces. Writing, cardboard, oak tag, newspaper, and other specialty papers can create unusual textures, designs, and patterns when applied in a variety of ways. Most art-supply stores carry specialty papers.

Chamois & Burlap: Chamois and burlap cloth can create exciting textures. Use folded or cut chamois to create specific shapes. Use burlap to add texture. Be creative and try out various other types of material.

Combs: Drag steel, rubber, or plastic combs through the paint or glaze to create grain lines that simulate different wood textures.

Look around your home. You'll find erasers, cork, cotton swabs, steel wool, pot scrubbers, squeegees, and a host of other things that can act as tools for creating unusual textures and finishes. Try experimenting.

the formula notebook

It's a good idea to keep notes on your faux-finishing or mural-painting project. These notes can become an excellent resource when looking back over past projects. If you ever need to repeat a finish, all the information is available. How many times have you wanted to redo something and forgot how you did it to begin with? A notebook is invaluable when mixing your own colors. You'll be happy you have a record.

Although most paint colors are available at paint or hardware stores, you may enjoy the fun and challenge of creating your own colors. Imagine coming up with a color nobody else seems to have.

Buy a spiral-bound notebook to record all your mixing formulas for colors and glazes and to record use of specialty tools and materials.

design tip
Use a hairdryer to speed up the drying process.

paint formulas & samples

Mixing colors is not difficult. First prepare sample boards. These will also help test faux-finish abilities. The boards can be illustration, oak-tag, or Bristol boards. I prefer the less expensive oak tag; it works just as well as other materials. Paint the board with the primer you've chosen for your project. One coat is sufficient. Then paint on the top-coat color. Allow each to dry thoroughly before applying the next. The oak tag will probably curl, but it should straighten out after it dries. Painting both sides of the oak tag may prevent it from curling. Find some clothes hangers, tape, and heavy string or wire. Attach the string to the wall like a clothesline. Be sure to keep it out of the traffic lanes in your home; you don't want anyone to walk into it. Attach one end of a strip of masking tape to the back of the oak tag. Loop the other end over the hanger. Let the oak-tag paint sample hang to dry.

Prepare enough boards so you can make as many samples as you need. I usually prepare 10 to 20 boards at a time. This sounds like a lot, but I put them aside for later projects.

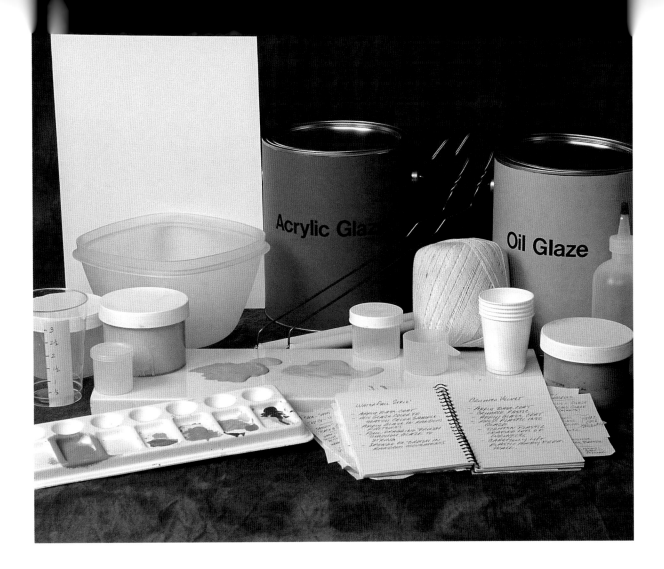

Here's the fun part: time to mix the paint. Fill a plastic container halfway up with a pure-white base coat.

Mix the paint in small amounts. A paper cup with inch or milliliter marks on the outside will help you to accurately record the amounts you mix. This will also be helpful for mixing larger amounts of paint.

When mixing colors and paint, I use a piece of marble as a surface since it does not absorb the paint. Plexiglas also works well.

Add only a few drops of color at a time when tinting. Stir the mixture thoroughly. Test the sample on a piece of the prepared board. Let it dry to see results. If you're satisfied with the color, mix enough for your project. Mix extra paint so that you don't run out halfway through the project. Of course, if you want a color that's on a paint chart, it would be more economical to buy paint already mixed.

design tip
You can use an old plastic milk or bleach bottle. Just cut off the top third. Clean it out thoroughly and you're ready.

If the color you mix is too bright, tone it down with a complementary color (the color that's opposite it on the color wheel). Don't use black because it will dull the color. Let's say you're making a light red. It turns too pink. You can tone it down by using some green (red is opposite green on the color wheel). If you plan to mix colors, be sure you have a color wheel.

glaze formulas & samples

Glazes follow a different formula. They don't require much coloring, since they are supposed to be transparent. Try only a few drops of color, and mix the glaze sample thoroughly. Then test it on a prepared board coated with the top-coat color that you'll use on the wall. This will give you the best visual results before you apply the glaze to the wall.

If you would prefer to mix your own glaze from scratch, here are some recipes.

Oil Glaze: Use 1 part linseed oil to 3 parts turpentine, and add a few drops of Japan drier.
Alkyd Glaze: Mix 1 part raw or boiled linseed oil, 1 part alkyd interior paint, and 1 part paint thinner.
To slow down the drying time, replace the 1 part paint thinner with 1/2 part thinner and 1/2 part kerosene.

Latex Glaze: Use 1 part vinyl wallpaper paste (premixed) and 1 part water. Glycerin can be added to slow down the drying time.

For those of you who want a commercial type of glaze, but who still like mixing your own, try these formulas.

Slightly Transparent Oil Glaze: Mix 3 parts mineral spirits to 1 part ready-made oil glaze. Add 2 to 3 tablespoons of white undercoat paint.

Basic Oil Glaze: Use 6 parts ready-made oil glaze to 1 part paint thinner.

Acrylic Glaze: The commercial product can be thinned with water, but it will dry quickly. Glycerin can be added to slow down the drying time.

When mixing samples, always have sufficient lighting. This should be daylight or color-corrected light. For best results, mix and view these samples in the room where you are decorating. So try various combinations; mix away and enjoy.

traditional faux
finishes

a **wide variety of** faux finishes have been around for many years. It's quite possible that your great-grandfather or great-grandmother created faux finishes at home. If you've never painted faux finishes before, we'll help you get started. Of course, if you feel more daring, turn to the "Innovative Faux Finishes" chapter. Whatever finish you choose, keep in mind that this is supposed to be fun.

sponging

Sponging is the easiest decorative finish to master. You can sponge with paint or tinted glaze on a color base. Depending on the base, the texture can be transparent, very crisp, or soft and slightly blended. You can have a variety by using one, two, or more colors. Try one color on top of another to give it some depth. If you use latex paint, each layer will dry quickly. Oil (alkyd) paint will take much longer to dry.

If you sponge in a random pattern, the finished wall will look much more attractive. This means that you need to change the position of your hand and sponge while working to avoid a repetitious sponge pattern. Let enough of the base color show through when sponging on the color.

First wet the sponge and thoroughly squeeze out the excess water. Keep a bucket of water handy to rinse out any built-up paint or glaze. Next pour the paint or glaze into a roller tray.

Before proceeding to the wall, practice your sponge imprint on a piece of oak tag or cardboard. This will give you a feel for handling the sponge. It will also show you how much paint and pressure to apply to the surface. Once you are satisfied with your results you can begin to work on the wall. While you are sponging, step back every now and then to observe your progress. Remember to take your time; there's no need to rush.

Materials

Paint or glaze
Masking tape
Roller tray or large container
Large sea sponge
Drop cloth

step 1 Choose the wall(s) you want to sponge. With masking tape, tape off areas you don't want sponged.

step 2 Use rubber gloves to keep the paint off your hands. Wet the sponge with water and ring it out thoroughly. Then dip the sponge into the paint. Drag it across the edge of the tray to remove excess paint. Dab the sponge on a piece of paper to eliminate any blobbing.

step 3 Lightly touch the sponge to the wall. Don't squeeze or press the sponge too hard. This will cause blobs or runs. Don't worry if you make a mistake; just wash it off immediately and redo that section. Move your *wrist* to keep from repeating the same pattern. *Turn* the sponge for more pattern variation. As the sponge runs low on paint or glaze, increase pressure on the wall. Renew the paint when necessary.

step 4 Use the edge of a large sponge or choose a smaller sponge to get into corners.

step 5 When you are finished, you won't be able to tell how many times the sponge has touched the wall. Consider these steps a guide. Do what appeals to you. If you don't like it, paint over the wall and begin again.

step 6 Clean all equipment with the proper solvents. See the "Faux Media & Finishes" chapter.

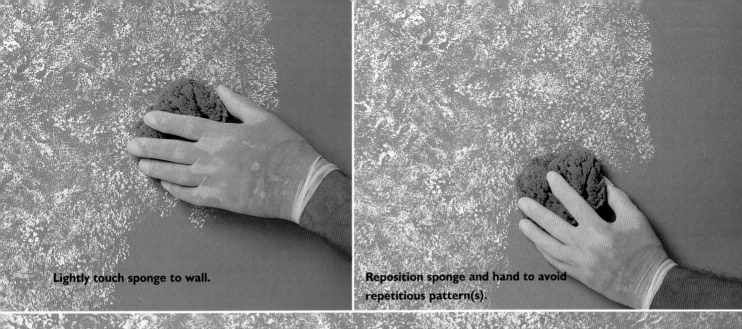

Lightly touch sponge to wall.

Reposition sponge and hand to avoid repetitious pattern(s).

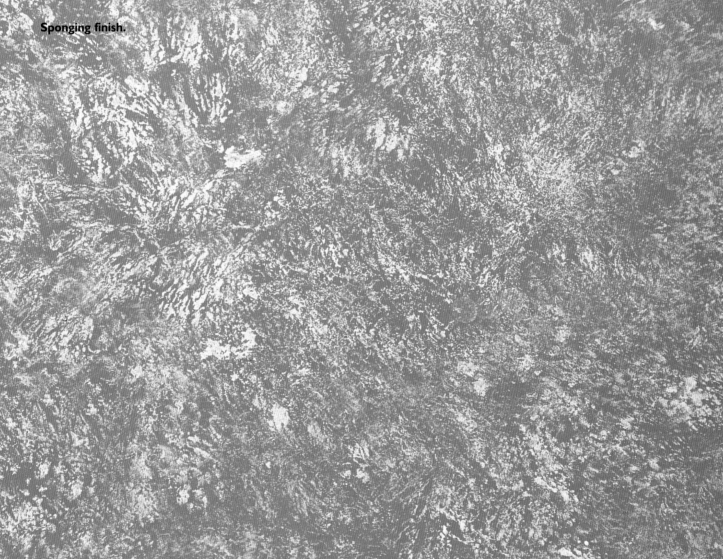

Sponging finish.

sponging off

Sponging off is a faux-finishing technique similar to sponging. However, for sponging off, first you apply the paint or glaze on the walls, then you remove it with the sponge before it dries. This is achieved by pressing the sponge into the medium. As you remove the sponge from the wall, dip it in solvent to remove the excess medium. Squeeze out any excess solvent and continue pressing until you are happy with the results.

If you're using latex, work in small (4 x 4-foot) sections because the paint dries quickly. You can work larger areas by using alkyd paint or glaze. Alkyd paint and glaze dry much more slowly, allowing more workable time. Choose the paint you favor for a slower or faster drying time. Review the drying times in the "Faux Media & Finishes" chapter.

step 1 Apply the base-coat color and allow it to dry thoroughly.

step 2 Paint the wall with the paint or glaze using a brush or roller. Work in small sections (about 4 x 4 feet), applying a light, even coat.

step 3 Wet the sea sponge and ring it out thoroughly. Then press it into the wet paint or glaze and pull it away from the wall. If the base coat is not showing through, press harder. Move quickly, but don't rush. Rinse the sponge out in a bucket of water (for latex) or paint thinner (for alkyd). Continue pressing until enough of the base coat and top coat is showing.

step 4 After the paint or glaze is dry, you can apply a second color on top of the first, if desired. Just follow the same procedure.

step 5 Clean all equipment with the proper solvents. See the "Faux Media & Finishes" chapter.

Press the sea sponge to the wall to remove paint.

Reposition sea sponge in hand to avoid repetitious pattern(s).

Sponging-off finish.

Ragging is a faux-finishing technique that's a little different than sponging. After you try it, you'll want to rag everything. The paint applicator is a rag and not a sponge.

Materials

Paint or glaze

Masking tape

Roller tray or large container

Large lint-free cotton rag (12 x 12 inches or larger)

Drop cloth

Bucket

step 1 Apply the base-coat color.

step 2 Pour the paint or glaze into a large container (large enough for you to dip in both the rag and your hand) or roller tray. Wear rubber gloves to keep the paint off your hands.

step 3 Dip the cotton rag into the container and wring it out. Don't squeeze it too much or the rag will be too dry. Bunch up the rag and tuck the corners inside. Leave enough ridges and grooves in the material. Don't make it flat. These ridges and grooves create the surface. Then press the rag on a piece of oak tag or cardboard to check the results. If you are satisfied with the pattern, you can continue to the next step.

step 4 Lightly press the rag to the wall. Lift the rag cleanly away from the wall. Press again in an adjacent area. Move your wrist and change the position of the rag from time to time. This will help vary the pattern.

  Stand back every now and then to review your progress. You should work quickly, but carefully before the medium dries. Remember if you are not satisfied with the results, you can paint over the finish and start again.

design tip
Use a toothpick to remove any loose rag fibers in the finish. If you press your fingers into the paint, you could mar the finish.

step 5 Clean all equipment with the proper solvents. See the "Faux Media & Finishes" chapter.

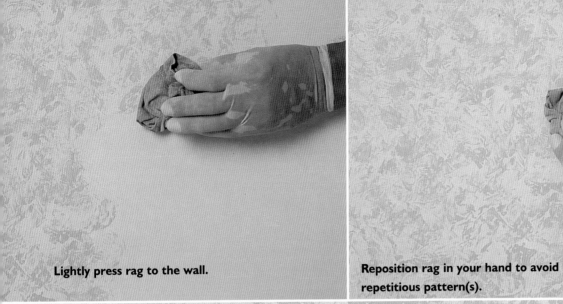

Lightly press rag to the wall.

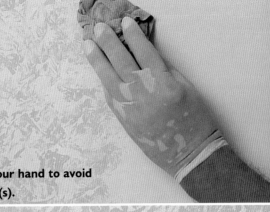

Reposition rag in your hand to avoid repetitious pattern(s).

Ragging finish.

Ragging off is a faux-finishing technique similar to sponging off. First you apply paint or glaze to the surface with a brush or roller; then you remove it with a cotton rag.

Materials

Paint or glaze

Masking tape

Roller tray or large container

Large lint-free cotton rag (12 x 12 inches or larger)

Drop cloth

step 1 Paint the wall with paint or glaze using a brush or roller. Work in small sections (about 4 x 4 feet), applying a light, even coat.

step 2 Use a square 12 x 12-inch cotton rag. Bunch up the rag and tuck the corners inside. Leave enough ridges and grooves; these create the surface. Press the rag into the wet paint or glaze and pull it away from the wall. If the base coat is not showing through, press harder. Rearrange the rag to alter the pattern. Rinse the excess medium out of the rag into a bucket of water (for latex) or paint thinner (for alkyd). Continue rearranging and pressing the rag until you're satisfied with the results.

step 3 After the paint or glaze is dry, you can apply a second color if desired.

step 4 Clean all equipment with the proper solvents. See the "Faux Media & Finishes" chapter.

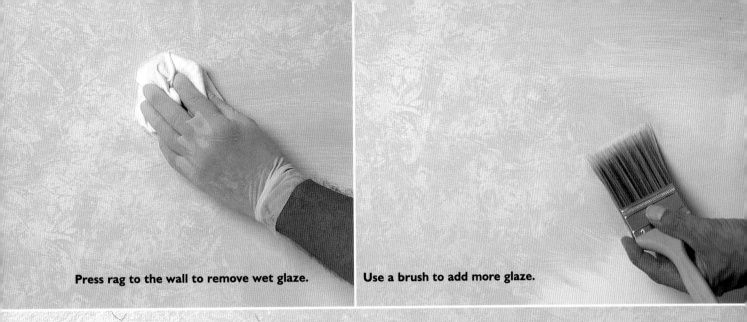

Press rag to the wall to remove wet glaze.

Use a brush to add more glaze.

Ragging-off finish.

rag rolling

Rag rolling is similar to ragging, except the shape of the rag and the way it's manipulated are key to the success of this technique. This technique is something like using a rolling pin. Hold the rag in both hands and roll it onto the wall. The paint is deposited from the rag to the wall.

Materials

Paint or glaze
Masking tape
Roller tray or large container
Large lint-free cotton rag (12 x 12 inches or larger)
Drop cloth

step 1 Saturate the cotton rag with paint or glaze and squeeze out any excess. You don't want the rag to drip. Fold it in half and roll it loosely into a tube shape.

step 2 Work the wall from the top down to the bottom. Place the rag against the wall with both hands. Roll the rag evenly. When it unrolls, remove the rag from the wall, roll it up again, and continue. The next row should touch the previous row. As the paint or glaze fades, re-dip the rag, wring it out, and continue working carefully before the medium dries.

step 3 Clean any drips or equipment with the proper solvents. See the "Faux Media & Finishes" chapter.

Roll the rag evenly down the wall.

Rag-rolling finish.

Rag rolling off is a faux-finishing technique that combines rag rolling and sponging off wall sections, thereby removing the finish.

Materials

Paint or glaze
Masking tape
Roller tray or large container
Large lint-free cotton rag (12 x 12 inches or larger)
Drop cloth

step 1 Working in small sections (about 4 x 4 feet), apply the top coat of paint or glaze. Fold the square cotton cloth in half and roll it loosely into a tube shape. Roll the tube-shaped rag on the wall to remove some of the medium.

step 2 Work the wall from the top down to the bottom. Place the rag against the wall with both hands. Roll the rag evenly. When it unrolls, remove the rag from the wall, roll it up again, and continue. The next row should touch the previous row. As the paint or glaze fades, re-dip the rag, wring it out, and continue working carefully before the medium dries.

step 3 As the rag accumulates the medium, rinse it off in the proper solvent. See the "Faux Media & Finishes" chapter. Continue rolling the rag, working carefully but quickly before the medium dries.

Roll rag down the wall to remove wet glaze.

Add more glaze with a brush.

Rag-rolling-off finish.

strié **(stree-ay)** **is** a French term meaning "striated" or a "scratched-glaze surface." This technique produces a classic, elegant appearance when produced with subtle colors. It produces a grand, festive appearance when created with bright and bold colors. Are you classic or grand? The strié effect is achieved with a dry brush pulled or dragged through a layer of wet glaze. The brush is called a flogger or dragger. Many other tools, such as cardboard and steel or rubber combs, also work well.

Materials

Glaze (alkyd or latex) & glaze colors
Flogger or dragger brush
Masking tape (to protect unpainted areas)
Absorbent rags
Guide stick (1- to 2-inch-wide knot-free pine board) cut to length or width of wall
Small level (attach to guide stick for horizontal lines)
Handle (attach to guide stick for easy handling)

step 1 Mask off the areas you don't want painted. Apply the base coat and let it dry.

step 2 Begin at the ceiling and work down to the floor. Brush or roll on a wide section of glaze. Work in a 6-foot width. Then lightly brush or roll out the excess glaze on the outside edge, leaving a wet edge.

step 3 Start at the top. Pull the brush downward, following the corner edge. Work your way to the floor. You may need a stepladder to reach the ceiling. Walk down the steps of the ladder while you drag the brush through the glaze. If you aren't able to go the full length, you can feather out your strokes just below eye level. Start your next stroke just above your stopping point. Follow the same lines to the bottom.

design tip
To feather, brush and lift the brush off the surface to avoid a hard line.

step 4 As you get close to the wet edge, brush on a new section of glaze as described in step 2. To keep the pattern straight, just follow a line in the previously dragged section. Continue until you have completed the whole wall.

Remove excess paint by wiping the brush on a rag or newspaper. Even the excess glaze that collects on the floor molding can be easily removed. How? Just rap a piece of cloth around a spackling knife and pull the edge through the excess glaze. This will allow the collected glaze to be removed without disturbing the finish. Wipe off the excess on a rag or newspaper and you're almost finished.

step 5 Clean all equipment with the proper solvents. See the "Faux Media & Finishes" chapter.

Apply glaze to wall.

Pull brush down to form a strié pattern.

Strié finish.

innovative **faux**
finishes

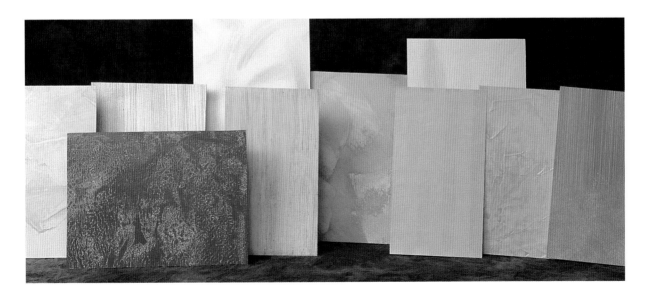

Some of these innovative faux finishes are alterations of old faux finishes and some are new. I discovered them while working on other projects. I guess that's why I always emphasize the word *experiment*. Coming up with new faux finishes can even happen by mistake. The only problem is to try to remember how it happened. That's why it's also important to take notes while working on the finishes.

This is a great technique that can give any room in your home the look and charm of an old villa located in a mountainside village. It can give the look of decades without the flaking and crumbling that is associated with an aging painted surface.

Materials

Base-coat color
Paintbrush (for applying color)
Paintbrush (for dry brushing)
Top-coat paint or glaze
Masking tape (to protect unpainted areas)

The base color should complement or coordinate with the top coat. Refer to the color wheel and choose colors that will enhance the room you are decorating.

step 1 Apply your base coat and let it thoroughly dry.

step 2 Mix the top-coat paint or glaze, depending on the finish you require. The paint will give a soft matte finish. Thin the paint with water for a washlike finish. The glaze will have a glossy sheen; tint the glaze as explained in the "Faux Media & Finishes" chapter.

step 3 Apply the paint or glaze with a brush, in a hit-and-miss pattern. Work in 6 x 6-foot sections because you will be removing some of the paint before it dries.

step 4 Remove some of the wet paint with a dry brush. You may have to press hard to remove the paint. Leave any visible brush strokes. Blend in some areas.

step 5 Clean all equipment with the proper solvents. See the "Faux Media & Finishes" chapter.

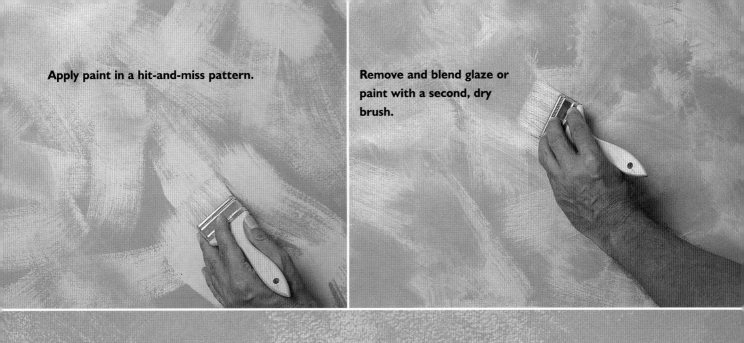

Apply paint in a hit-and-miss pattern.

Remove and blend glaze or paint with a second, dry brush.

Old World finish.

bamboo-cloth strié

This faux finish simulates bamboo cloth. The steps are the same as for the strié technique, except that instead of a brush you use a rust-resistant scrubbing pad.

Materials

Glaze (oil or latex)

Glaze colors

Rust-resistant scrubbing pad

Masking tape (to protect unpainted areas)

Absorbent rags

Guide stick (1- to 2-inch-wide knot-free pine board) cut to length or width of wall

Small level (attach to guide stick for horizontal lines)

Handle (attach to guide stick for easy handling)

step 1 Mask off areas that you don't want painted. Apply the base coat and let it dry. Fill a bucket with water and keep it handy to frequently rinse out built-up glaze from the pad.

step 2 It's best to begin at the ceiling and work down to the floor. Brush or roll on a wide section of glaze. Work in a 6-foot width. Then lightly brush out the excess glaze on the outside edge, leaving a wet edge.

step 3 Start at the top. Pull the pad downward, following the corner edge. You may need a stepladder to reach the ceiling. Work your way down to the floor. While dragging the pad, slightly shift it to the left or right to give an uneven look, which is what you want. Walk down the steps of the ladder while you drag the pad through the glaze. If you aren't able to go the full length, begin your next stroke just above your stopping point. Follow the same lines to the bottom. Rinse out the pad in the bucket to remove built-up glaze.

step 4 As you get close to the wet edge, brush on a new section of glaze. To keep the pattern straight, follow a line in the previously dragged section. Continue until you have completed the whole wall.

Excess paint can be removed by wiping the brush on a rag or newspaper. Even the excess glaze that collects on the floor molding can be easily removed. How? Just rap a piece of cloth around a spackling knife and pull the edge through the excess glaze. This will allow collected glaze to be removed without disturbing the finish. Wipe off the excess on a rag or newspaper and you're almost finished.

step 5 Clean all equipment with the proper solvents. See the "Faux Media & Finishes" chapter.

Add glaze to the wall using a brush.

Drag a scrubbing pad down through the wet glaze.

For bamboo-cloth strié, slightly shift pad left or right at uneven intervals.

iridescent strié

The steps are the same as those in the strié technique (p. 82), except that you mix an iridescent medium into the glaze. See the "Special Effects Media" chapter. The medium will give your finish a more shimmering and elegant effect. This iridescent glaze can also be used as a top coat on other finishes.

Materials

Glaze (oil or latex)

Glaze colors

Flogger or dragger brush

Masking tape (to protect unpainted areas)

Absorbent rags

Guide stick (1- to 2-inch-wide knot-free pine board) cut to length or width of wall

Small level (attach to guide stick for horizontal lines)

Handle (attach to guide stick for easy handling)

strié waterfall

This variation on the standard strié pattern can give your wall the appearance of a waterfall. The first steps are the same as those for the strié technique above; then you add a few more steps.

Materials

Glaze (oil or latex)

Glaze colors

Flogger or dragger brush

Color chalk

Masking tape (to protect unpainted areas)

Absorbent rags

Guide stick (1- to 2-inch-wide knot-free pine board) cut to length or width of wall

Small level (attach to guide stick for horizontal lines)

Handle (attach to guide stick for easy handling)

Iridescent strié finish.

step 1 Mask off the areas that you don't want painted. Apply the base coat and let it dry.

step 2 Begin at the ceiling and work down to the floor. Brush or roll on a wide section of glaze. Work in a 6-foot width. Then lightly brush out excess glaze on the outside edge, leaving a wet edge.

step 3 Mark the wall on opposite ends. Use chalk to mark the halfway (or less if desired) point between the floor and ceiling.

step 4 Brush or roll on a wide section of glaze from the ceiling to the halfway mark. Lightly brush out the excess glaze, leaving a wet edge.

step 5 Start at the top. Pull the brush downward, following the corner edge. You may need a stepladder to reach the ceiling. Walk down the steps of the ladder while you drag the brush through the glaze. If you aren't able to go the full length, feather out your strokes just below eye level. Then begin the next stroke just slightly inside the finished area. Follow the same lines to the bottom. Work your way down to the string. Complete the top section of the wall first.

step 6 Now you can apply the glaze to the bottom section (below the chalk mark). This is the fun part. Take your brush and swirl and dab it through the glaze. You want the swirling to suggest the churning water at the bottom of a waterfall.

design tip
You can replace the brush with a sea sponge.

Make sure you brush out the glaze as much as possible on the halfway point so you don't get a hard line.

Remove excess paint by wiping the brush on a rag or newspaper. Even the excess glaze that collects on the floor molding can be easily removed. Wrap a piece of cloth around a spackling knife and pull the edge through the excess glaze. This will allow collected glaze to be removed without disturbing the finish. Wipe off the excess on a rag or newspaper and you're almost finished.

step 7 Clean all equipment with the proper solvents. See the "Faux Media & Finishes" chapter.

Brush on glaze above chalk mark.

Brush on wet glaze.

Below chalk mark, swirl and dab brush through wet glaze for strié waterfall.

color layering

This creative finish is a little time-consuming, but it can give your walls or ceiling a combination of Old World charm and New Age elegance. The most important part is to choose colors that work well together. Decide what base-coat color and top-coat color you want before you begin. You could, for instance, pick up a color from your furnishings or introduce a second color to your decorative scheme. If you're still having a color dilemma, refer to the "Color Palette" chapter.

Materials

Primer (latex or alkyd)
Spackle (available at paint or hardware stores)
Spackling knife (width depends on project size)
Sandpaper (200–400-grit nonclogging)
Base- and top-coat paint colors
Paintbrush or paint roller and tray
Masking tape (to protect unpainted areas)

step 1 Paint on your base-coat color and allow it to dry thoroughly.

step 2 Apply Spackle to your wall with a spackling knife. Don't put too much Spackle on the blade. Use small amounts until you become familiar with the technique. If you're not sure how to apply Spackle, practice on a piece of oak tag. Make short, scraping, hit-and-miss passes with the spackling knife. Allow enough of the base coat to show through. Discard any Spackle on the knife that you don't use on the wall. Always keep the Spackle container tightly covered.

Place the blade against the inside edge when spackling corners. Work the blade outward, toward the center of the wall. Allow the Spackle to dry according to the manufacturer's specifications.

step 3 Once the Spackle is dry, you can lightly sand down any peaks and high spots. The surface should be somewhat level but still contain enough ridges. These ridges will hold the second color in place. After you sand, wipe the surface clean of Spackle dust with a damp cloth, and let it dry. Clean the spackling knife with water and dry. You'll need the knife for the next step.

step 4 Dip the spackling blade into the top-coat paint. Be careful not to get too much on the blade or it will drip. Quickly apply the paint with the same hit-and-miss scraping passes as you did the Spackle. Allow the paint to accumulate in the ridges. Be sure that enough of the base coat and

Apply Spackle with spackling knife.

Sand down any high spots.

Apply paint color with spackling knife.

some of the Spackle coat show through the top coat. If there's too much paint in any area, just re-scrape with the knife to remove the excess. Step back from the wall every now and then to observe your progress.

step 5 Allow the surface to dry thoroughly. You're finished! You can apply another coat of paint if desired.

step 6 Clean all equipment with the proper solvents. See the "Faux Media & Finishes" chapter.

Color-layering finishes.

metallic-color layering

The steps are the same as for the color-layering technique, except the top coat is a metallic paint, such as gold, bronze, or silver, depending on your particular decor. This will give a more industrial or futuristic look to your room. Some metallic colors may be expensive. To reduce the expense, add more volume to the paints by mixing in some glaze medium.

Materials

Primer (latex or alkyd)

Spackle

Spackling knife (width depends on project size)

Sandpaper (200–400-grit nonclogging)

Metallic paint color

Paintbrush or paint roller and tray

Masking tape (to protect unpainted areas)

Metallic-color-layering finish.

This can create an elegant and formal or fun and exciting room. It can also create the appearance of striped wallpaper. I painted a hallway with this finish and people thought it was actual wallpaper. The basic striping steps are the same. The technique described here will give you a tone-on-tone stripe.

Materials

Base-coat paint

Nonyellowing polyurethane
(for the tone-on-tone only)

Masking tape

Measuring tape

Plumb line (a string with a weight
attached to the bottom)

Mini-roller (optional)

Sponge brush (optional)

Paintbrush

step 1 First decide if you want an even range of stripes on your wall. If so, start from the center. If it doesn't matter, you can start from either end.

step 2 Determine the width of the stripes you want. They can be 1, 2, or 3 inches wide. The space between the stripes can be wider or of equal width. Equal width is easier, because you can use a width of masking tape that's equal to your space. For example, if you have a 2-inch space, use a 2-inch-wide masking tape.

step 3 **Starting from the Center:** Measure and mark the center of the wall with a pencil. Use tick (pencil-point) marks and not a solid line. Pencil lines have a tendency to come through the paint. Then use a plumb line or level and mark a vertical line with a pencil. After you've decided the width of your stripe, divide that number in half. Then mark that measurement on each side of the central line to indicate your first stripe.

Starting from the Edge: Measure the width of the first stripe. Now indicate a vertical line with pencil-tick marks.

Various stripe widths.

Use pencil tick marks for stripe widths.

Pattern with centered stripe.

Pattern starting at left corner.

step 4 Apply the masking tape to areas you don't want painted. Keep the tape straight and burnish down the edge only. This will keep the paint from creeping under the tape, giving you a rough and unsightly edge. Continue along the wall and place the tape at the proper intervals. Any paint that creeps under the tape can be touched up after it dries.

design tip
You do not have to tape the whole wall because the tape can be reused.

step 5 Apply a nonyellowing polyurethane with a sponge brush, small roller, or paintbrush to the exposed areas.

step 6 When the polyurethane is thoroughly dry, carefully remove the masking tape. Continue on to the next section or sit back and enjoy your finish.

step 7 Clean all equipment with the proper solvent. See the "Faux Media & Finishes" chapter.

stripe variations

The steps are the same as for creating stripes. The only difference is that you will be using sponges, rags, iridescent gel, or metallic paint instead of polyurethane. You can also use color-on-color—say, a medium green on a light-green base, or whatever color enhances your décor. These stripes can also be painted on only the lower half of the wall. This nice effect will be similar to a wainscoting. Be creative! Try variations with the widths and finishes.

Press edges of tape to the wall.

Glazed stripes.

This is a fun technique that can give some very unique finishes and textures. You can accomplish this by simply pressing various types of paper into wet paint or glaze and removing. You can use oak tag, onionskin, tracing, acetate, vellum, and any other papers. Use your imagination and try pressing one type of paper into the wet medium, then a different type on top of the first one. Each pattern will be different from the next.

Materials

Paper (various types in at least
    8½ × 11-inch sheets or larger)
Base-coat paint color
Glaze or paint top-coat color
Rubber gloves
Masking tape (to protect unpainted
    areas)

step 1   Decide on your base color and paint the wall(s). Now choose the top-coat color or glaze tint.

step 2 Next pick the type of paper you want to use. Be sure you have enough sheets for the area you are working. You can determine the amount by figuring that heavier paper will hold together much longer after being pressed into the wet surface a few times.

step 3 Apply the paint or tinted glaze to the wall in small 6 × 6-foot sections. Remember if you are using latex paint to work quickly before the paint dries. Of course, you can apply more paint or glaze if it has dried.

step 4 Before pressing the paper into the glaze, fold up one corner. This fold is a grab corner so you can remove the paper from the wall without marring the surface with your fingertips. You don't

Press paper into wet glaze.

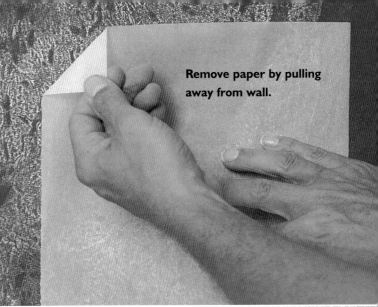

Remove paper by pulling away from wall.

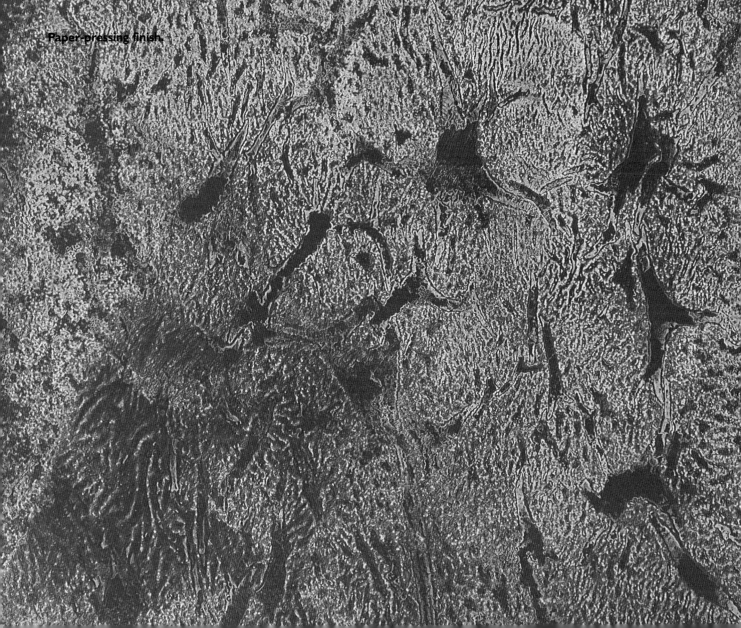

Paper-pressing finish.

want fingerprints in the finish! Press the paper into the wet medium. Now peel the paper back away. If you are satisfied with the results, you can continue. Or, press the paper again to remove even more of the medium. Slightly overlap each paper to avoid a block look (unless that's what you want). Continue overlapping until the whole wall is completed.

step 5 Clean all equipment with the proper solvents. See the "Faux Media & Finishes" chapter.

A variety of paper-pressing finishes made with different types of paper.

Brush swirling is relatively simple. All you do is lightly pull and drag a brush through a wet glaze surface. Think of yourself as a bandleader while moving the brush around in the glaze. This technique can be accomplished with a standard paintbrush or a dragging brush. It will require at least two colors. The best results will be with a pale or pastel base coat and a darker top coat. Or you can reverse the colors. Experimentation is the key to success.

Materials

Glaze (alkyd or latex)
Paint colors: base color and 2 colors for swirling
Standard or dragger brush
1- to 2-inch paintbrushes
Masking tape (to protect unpainted areas)

step 1 Choose the base color and two more colors. The two colors are for the swirling technique. If you're not sure what colors to choose, review the "Color Palette" chapter.

step 2 Apply a coat of glaze to the wall. Then apply a dollop of paint—by dipping the 1-inch brush into the paint—to the glaze. Follow with the other color. Place the dollops in random locations in the glaze.

step 3 Let your brush flow on the surface as you manipulate the dollop in a swirling pattern of curves and shapes through the glaze. Loosen up. Think about the water, wind, and even the clouds to help your brush flow. Add as much color as you like to the wall. If the glaze dries, it's OK because you can add more over the dried glaze.

step 4 Clean all equipment with the proper solvents. See the "Faux Media & Finishes" chapter.

Add a clear glaze base; then add dollops of paint.

Brush and swirl through color.

Finished wall with brush swirling.

Brush-swirling finish.

faux wallpaper

You could search for days or even weeks and not find the type of wallpaper that best suits your décor. Why not make your own pattern or design? It's not difficult. No, you don't need a printing press. All you need is some imagination, a stencil, paper, paint, and glaze.

Materials

- Stencil paper, oak tag, or Bristol board
- Paint or stencil brush
- Glaze
- Paint
- Tape measure
- T-square or straightedge
- String (to align the design on large areas)
- Masking tape (to hold the stencil in place and to protect unpainted surfaces)
- Plumb bob or weighted string
- Carpenter's level

step 1 Choose the pattern or design for your wallpaper. Now figure out the number of colors you want to use. The library is an excellent source for books on patterns. Many designers, like me, go there quite often to do research. Once you've found the pattern you like, enlarge it on a photocopy machine. You may have to enlarge it a few times to get the size you require. Trace your design onto a sheet of oak tag, acetate, Mylar, or stencil paper. If you use oak tag, you will want to cover the front and back with a coat of shellac or lacquer. Do this before you cut

Draw a pattern on paper to visualize the design.

Trace the pattern onto tracing paper.

Transfer the pattern to a stencil.

Carefully cut out the stencil pattern.

out your pattern. This will keep the oak tag from falling apart from constant use. Allow the shellac to dry for at least an hour.

step 2 Decide how your pattern will repeat itself on the wall. First get a large sheet of paper and draw the pattern as you want it to appear on the wall. Remember that each color will require its own stencil, and each stencil must be registered to match the other stencil's color.

step 3 After you are satisfied with the pattern, tape the stencil paper to a cutting board. Then tape the photocopy on top of the stencil paper. First practice cutting out the pattern on a piece of scrap paper. Carefully cut out your design and alignment notches using a craft (X-acto) knife. Always use sharp blades, because a dull one will tear the stencil. Watch your fingertips. Be extra careful not to cut the thin areas that link the patterns together. Most mistakes can be corrected with masking tape.

Mark all stencils with the word *UP* and keep them numbered, if you have more than two, to avoid any confusion.

step 4 With a carpenter's level, mark the horizontal lines. Use chalk to make the lines; pencils and markers bleed through paint. Then mark the verticals using the plumb bob. Align the stencil to the marks on the wall. Attach the stencil to the wall with artist's repositionable spray or masking tape. (Masking tape is easy to remove.)

step 5 Carefully dab the color onto the stencil with a stencil brush or sponge. If you use a brushing motion, the paint will seep under the stencil. Press the bristles or sponge straight into the stencil. After the paint is dry, lift a corner of the stencil to check the color. You can use a hair dryer to speed up the drying process, but keep it moving back and forth. Very carefully remove the stencil. Any paint seepage can be touched up with the base color.

step 6 Once you have finished the first color, proceed to the next color. Finally clean off the chalk with a damp cloth.

step 7 There are two different top-coat finishes that you can use, depending on your preference.
Matte Finish: If you choose this finish then your project is complete.
Glaze Finish: This finish requires one more step. You have to apply a clear glaze, which you can apply with a roller. If you prefer to use a brush, smooth out any brush marks by lightly touching the surface with the bristles. You don't want brush strokes to overpower your finish.

step 8 Clean all equipment with the proper solvents. See the "Faux Media & Finishes" chapter.

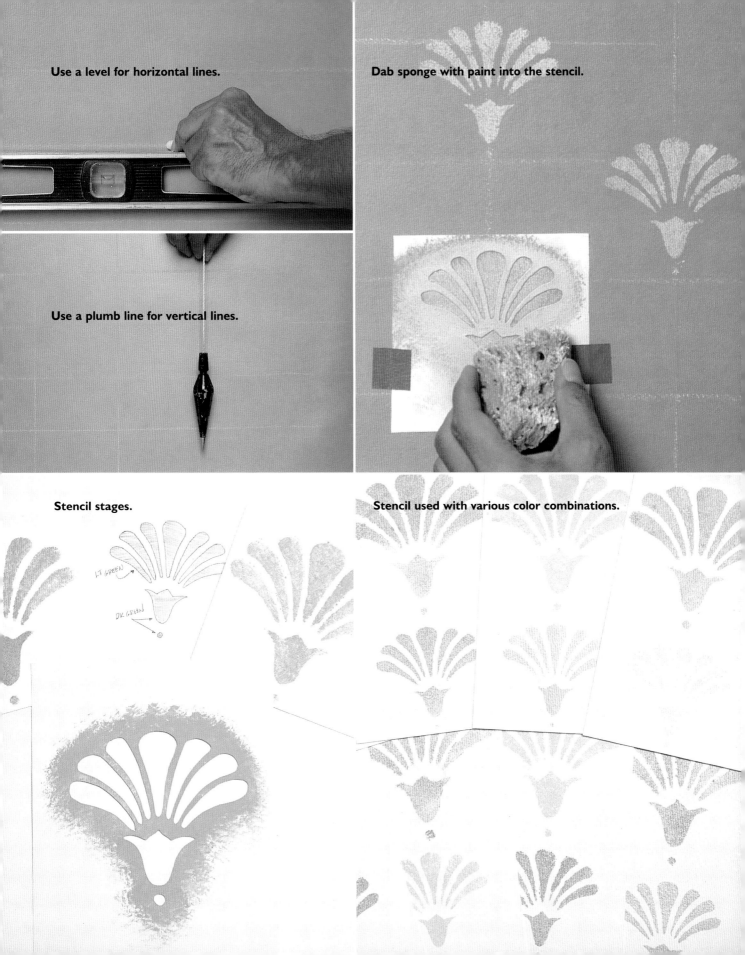

Use a level for horizontal lines.

Use a plumb line for vertical lines.

Dab sponge with paint into the stencil.

Stencil stages.

Stencil used with various color combinations.

Faux wallpaper (here and opposite page).

The rustic-walls finishing technique will lend walls the patina of age—a patina that normally only time could achieve. This technique is quick and easy. Just imagine, years of aging without waiting for them to pass. You can use almost any color, but warm colors will best suit this finish.

Materials

Base coat of semigloss or gloss paint
Paintbrush (for applying paint)
Top-coat paint (any sheen)
Lint-free cotton rags
Drop cloth

step 1 Decide on your base color and paint the wall(s). A semigloss or gloss base coat works best for this finish, since it's easier to combine and remove the paint over a shiny finish. Flat paints tend to absorb the top coat faster, allowing very little working time.

step 2 With the paintbrush loaded with paint, brush and spot on the top color in loose, random strokes. Leave a lot of the base-coat color showing and work in small areas. Work quickly so that the paint doesn't dry.

step 3 Apply the second coat in the same method as the first.

step 4 Now take a clean, lint-free rag and press it into paint. Turn and twist the rag to blend the colors together.

step 5 As the paint dries, rub off more of the top coat with the rag. Press hard to remove some areas of the top coat, leaving the base coat visible.

step 6 Clean all equipment with the proper solvents. See the "Faux Media & Finishes" chapter.

Apply first color.

Apply second color.

Blend colors together with a rag.

Rustic finish.

faux finishes for
wood **molding**

ecorative finishes for molding are often overlooked. This architectural element is used on the floor; around windows, doors, and ceilings; in corners; and as chair rails. Most of the time it is just painted white and tacked up—pretty boring. With the right paint and finish, any molding can be transformed into an eye-catching decoration.

These faux-finishing techniques are easy to apply. If the molding is attached, don't worry. Just use masking tape to keep paint off the walls. You'll find all the supplies at craft or hardware stores. The preparation is the same for each wood-molding faux technique.

Note: If you use gold leaf, the base coat will be different. Use rubber gloves and protect your eyes from any solvents.

For sponging, you'll need paint or glaze and a small sea sponge. You'll want the molding color to complement, or coordinate with, the walls.

Materials

Paint or glaze
Small sea sponges
Masking tape (for on-the-wall application)

step 1 Fill all imperfections in the molding with wood filler or Spackle. Prime knots with shellac or a stain sealer. Untreated knots will bleed through the paint and ruin the finish. If the molding is attached to the wall or ceiling, you can tape it off, using blue extended-release tape, then prime the molding.

step 2 Apply color using the sponge. Move and press the sponge into the grooves of the molding. Don't press too hard or you will get excess paint that will cause blobs and runs. If your paint blobs, correct it by wiping immediately with a damp cloth and re-pressing the sponge.

step 3 Allow the paint to dry before attaching the molding to the wall. After nailing, use a nail punch to set the nails. Fill the holes with a dab of Spackle. Wipe off the excess. Lightly sand and re-sponge the spackled area to make the nails invisible.

step 4 Clean all equipment with the proper solvents. See the "Faux Media & Finishes" chapter.

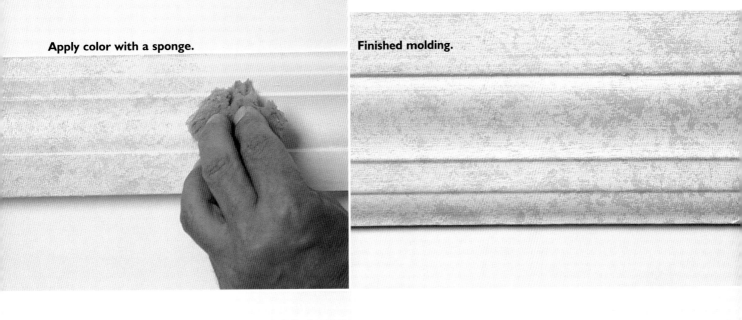

Apply color with a sponge.

Finished molding.

Two-color sponging techique on wood molding.

Sponging finish on wood molding.

This age-old technique will provide the rich look of gilded molding. This very desirable finish has been thought to be beyond most budgets. But it need not be. Here are a few different ways to obtain the effect of gold leaf.

The first way to achieve this finish is by applying a wax-based rub on the finish. Rub the medium with the fingers and then buff with a soft cloth to a lustrous finish. This can be applied quickly with little mess and it creates a very attractive finish.

The second method is to use real gold leaf. This is the most expensive and time-consuming method, but traditionalists favor it.

The third method is to use a high-grade gold paint and brush on the finish. Depending on your base-coat color, this finish will require two or three coats.

Materials

Gold

Gold-leaf gilding kit (for true gold leaf)

Gold size or Japan gold

or Rub 'n' Buff gold leaf (wax finish)

or Gold artist's acrylic paint

Other Items

Quality acrylic paintbrush

Blue extended-release tape

Primer for wood

White cotton cloths

gold-wax finish

step 1 Wear a rubber glove to apply the gold wax directly to the molding. Rub and smear the wax all over the molding.

step 2 Buff with a clean cotton cloth to a fine luster. Add more wax if necessary. After it dries it won't tarnish. This is an excellent less expensive substitution for genuine gold leaf.

step 3 Clean all equipment with the proper solvents. See the "Faux Media & Finishes" chapter.

Apply wax gold with your fingertip.

Buff with clean cloth to a fine luster.

Gold-wax finish on wood molding.

gold-leaf finish

step 1 Apply two coats of latex wood primer and allow to it dry. You can use white primer if you wish because gold leaf is translucent. Slide your fingertips over the wood. Is it rough? If so, lightly sand the wood. Don't press hard. Use a light touch since you don't want to remove the paint.

step 2 Apply a coat of gold size. Japan gold size works well on wood. The trick with the size is in determining the degree of tackiness. If the size is too dry, the leaf will not stick; if it's too wet, the leaf will wrinkle. How can you figure out the amount of time for the proper tackiness? Test the tackiness with your fingertip. If it slightly sticks to the size, you're ready to apply the leaf.

step 3 Remove a leaf of gold with the tissue from the booklet. Place the leaf carefully on the size. After you place the size it cannot be removed. Slightly overlap each leaf and keep all the leaves in the same direction. Press and smooth the leaf using the tissue. Any gaps can be filled in with gold-leaf scraps.

step 4 When the molding is covered with gold leaf, you can very carefully rub—in the direction of the overlaps—with a clean white cotton cloth. This will blend all the sheets together to form an even finish. Wasn't this easier than you originally thought?

step 5 Clean all equipment with the proper solvents. See the "Faux Media & Finishes" chapter.

gold-paint finish

step 1 Prime the wood with latex paint and allow it to dry.

step 2 Stir the gold paint thoroughly before and during use. This will keep the gold particles from separating and creating a watery finish.

step 3 Apply the paint in a smooth, flowing motion to give a uniform appearance. More than one coat will probably be necessary to achieve a deep gold finish.

step 4 Clean all equipment with the proper solvents. See the "Faux Media & Finishes" chapter.

Apply coat of gold size.

Apply gold leaf.

Carefully rub gold leaf with a clean white cloth.

Gold leaf on wood molding.

old world antiquing

Imagine having the look of aged antique moldings without the expense of the real thing. This finish is fun and easy to apply.

Materials

Silver paint
Wax-based gold paint
Black paint
Standard paintbrush (for applying paint or glaze)
Stiff paintbrush or stippling brush

step 1 Paint or spray the wood with a latex primer. Use two coats to allow minimal absorption of the top coat.

step 2 Apply a top coat of silver paint. Stir the paint before and during use. Use two top coats if desired. Allow each to dry thoroughly before applying the next.

step 3 Rub on small amounts of the wax-based gold paint. Use a hit-and-miss pattern. Apply the gold paint at random areas on the molding. Spread the gold thinly.

step 4 Stipple black paint into the recesses of the molding. Use a small paint or stipple brush. Leave the higher spots clear of the black paint. This will give the molding age and depth.

step 5 Clean all equipment with the proper solvents. See the "Faux Media & Finishes" chapter.

Prime wood and apply silver paint.

Apply small amounts of wax gold.

Stipple black paint into recesses.

Rub finish with clean cloth.

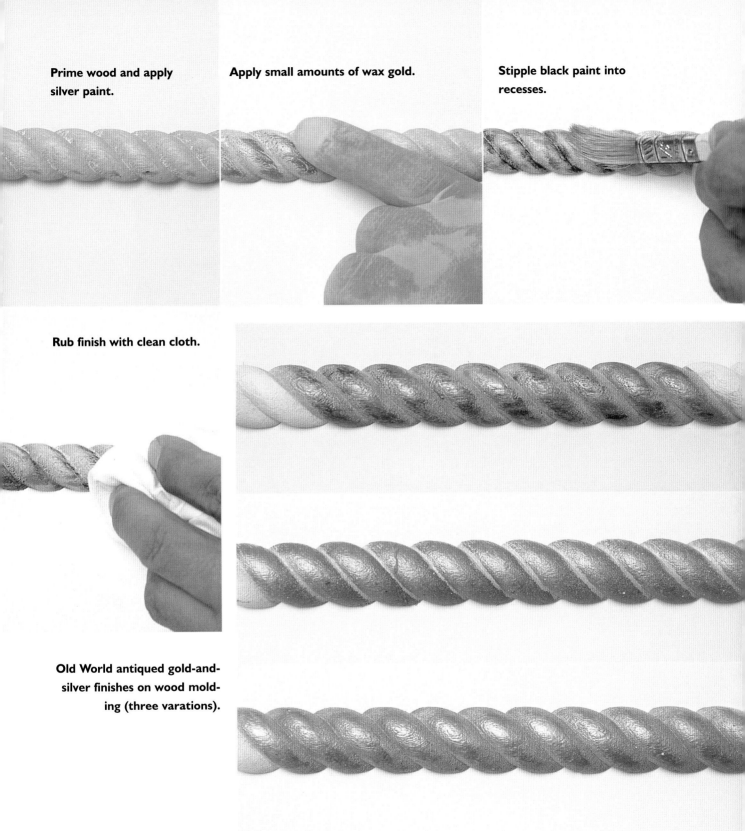

Old World antiqued gold-and-silver finishes on wood molding (three varations).

Stippling can add "age" to architectural elements. Use paint or glaze to achieve this look. First try it out on a small section of molding to determine the effect you desire.

Paint or glaze
Standard paintbrush (for applying paint or glaze)
Stiff paintbrush or stippling brush

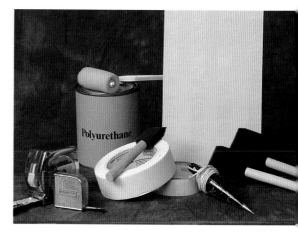

step 1 Apply the paint or glaze to the molding. Cover it completely. Brush into the deep carvings.

step 2 Dab a stiff brush or stippling brush into the wet glaze. This will remove some of the glaze onto the tips of the brush. Make a second pass if you want to remove more glaze. Be careful not to remove too much or it will get too light. Remove excess paint or glaze from the brush by dabbing it on a piece of newspaper or cardboard.

step 3 If you want to highlight the high-relief areas in the molding, follow this step. You can skip if you wish. First form a cotton rag into a square that's wide enough to completely cover the molding. Then carefully wipe along the molding. Use short passes. Remove only the paint on the high areas. If you press too hard, you'll remove all the glaze. Turn the rag frequently so that you don't redeposit paint on the molding.

step 4 Clean all equipment with the proper solvents. See the "Faux Media & Finishes" chapter.

Stipple brush into wet paint.

Wipe clean cloth over paint for highlights.

Strippled finish on wood molding.

This faux-finishing technique, wipe-on-off color, works well on high-relief or carved molding, since it enhances the molding's details. For best results, the molding should be free of nicks, scratches, knots, and holes.

Materials

Paint or glaze
1- to 2-inch paintbrush
Lint-free, absorbent cotton rags

step 1 Apply the paint or glaze, covering the molding. Make sure to get the paint inside all the grooves and carvings. Fold the cotton rag into a square or another shape or size your hand can handle.

step 2 Drag the rag lightly across the molding surface to remove the paint from the high spots. You want to remove the paint only from the raised areas and allow the deep recesses to retain the color.

step 3 Allow the paint or glaze to dry. Apply the color again if the effect is not dramatic enough.

step 4 Clean all equipment with the proper solvents. See the "Faux Media & Finishes" chapter.

design tip

Aluminum paint also acts as an excellent sealer. The pigment in aluminum paint consists of tiny ground flat-plate shapes. This seals the surface and keeps any sap from bleeding through to the surface. Remember to keep stirring well before and during use and to apply it with a brush. Cover just the knots and feather the strokes away from the knot. This will avoid a hard edge from showing through top coats.

treating knots

When painting wood you'll probably encounter knots. Seal any knots before continuing with priming or base coating. Shellac is a good sealer for knots; it's available in clear (dries transparent), blond (dries with an orange tint), and white. When buying shellac, always check the expiration date on the bottom of the can. Outdated shellac will not perform properly. Always keep the can tightly closed to prevent drying problems and "blooming," which causes a white haze.

Brush the shellac on the knot. Feather your strokes outward to achieve a smooth blend with the surrounding surface. Check the label for the drying time, which will vary with climate, location, and temperature.

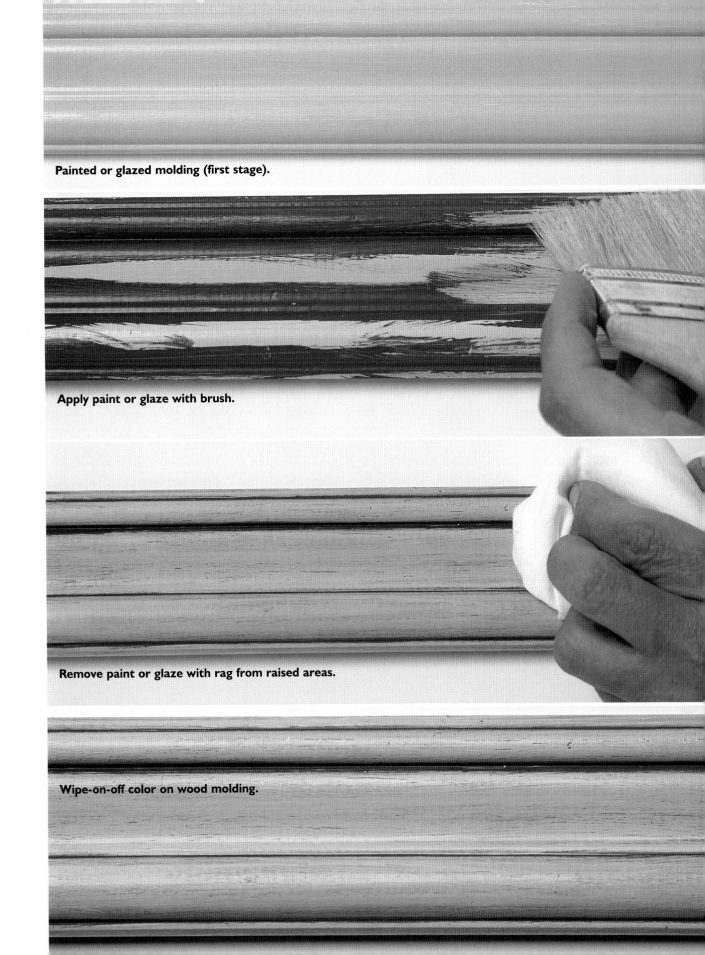

Painted or glazed molding (first stage).

Apply paint or glaze with brush.

Remove paint or glaze with rag from raised areas.

Wipe-on-off color on wood molding.

work checklist

Photocopy this checklist and use one or more for each project. We've left room for you to add more items.

technique

paint colors

BASIC EQUIPMENT

- Spackle and Spackling Knife
- Sandpaper
- Sanding Block
- Hammer (for molding)
- Finish Nails (for molding)
- Stepladder
- Masking Tape
- Drop Cloth
- Extension Cord
- Cotton Rags
- Trash Bags
- Portable Lighting
- Notebook or File Cards

PAINTING EQUIPMENT

- Paintbrushes
- Rollers
- Roller Tray
- Roller Extension
- Primer
- Base-Coat Paint
- Bucket
- Paint Strainer
- Specialty Tools

- Specialty Brushes

SAFETY EQUIPMENT

- Respirator Mask
- Rubber Gloves
- Portable Fan
- Folding Table or Workbench

PAINT MIXING EQUIPMENT

- Empty Paint Cans and Lids
- Stirring Sticks
- Solvents
- Mixing Cups
- Oak Tag or Bristol Boards
- Paint Strainers
- Large Paint-Mixing Containers

project notes

glossary

Absorption a process in which a liquid or gas is drawn into pores of a solid, porous material

Acetate clear plastic sheeting available in rolls or sheets and various thicknesses

Achromatic Colors white, black, grays, and silver

Acrylic Paint a water-based paint; durable, quick-drying, superior color, flexible, resistant to sunlight; available in tubes, jars, and other containers; dries to a matte finish; used for tinting base coats, painting murals, and creating faux finishes; the vehicle is acrylic resin, usually pigmented

Alkyd Paint a hard top-coat oil paint; thinned with paint thinner or turpentine; alkyd paint thinners are flammable

Aluminum Paint an excellent sealer for knots in wood; stir continuously during use

American Country a traditional style favoring bright, warm colors

American Southwest a traditional style favoring bright colors with black

Analogous Colors colors close to each other on the color wheel

Antiqued a term applied to a faux finish that suggests age

Artist's Oils good-quality durable paints with high oil content; blend easily, dry to semigloss sheen; paint thinner or turpentine required for cleanup

Arts & Crafts a style favoring greens, blues, browns, copper, and bronze

Badger-Bristle a brush made of badger hair that can be used with oil and water media; used for softening brush marks and graining

Bamboo-Cloth Strié a faux-finishing strié technique, using a scrubbing pad, that simulates bamboo cloth

Base Coat a coat of paint that helps cover a surface and hide flaws before the top coat is applied; *see also* Primer

Baseboard wooden molding or trim covering the joint of a wall and the adjoining floor

Bloom a white haze (usually undesirable) created when expired shellac is applied to a surface

Blue Extended-Release Tape usually blue tape, sold in 1- to 2-inch widths that can, e.g., be left on a surface for as many as several days without damaging the surface or leaving residue

Brush Painting coating a surface with paint using a paintbrush of synthetic or natural bristles

Brush Swirling a faux-finishing technique of applying two or more paints in a swirling fashion with a brush over wet glaze

Casein water-soluble paint when wet or dry; similar to watercolor but more opaque because of its white pigment; cover with a layer of shellac

Chair Rail a wood strip, trim, or molding around a wall; near the top of a chair back

Chart Tape used for special effects; tape is available in $1/64$- to 1-inch widths

Climate the average rainfall, humidity, and temperature of a locale, to be considered before applying paint or glaze to a surface and calculating drying time

Color-Corrected Light a special light source that allows colors to be viewed in natural light

Color Layering a faux-finishing technique that uses one base-coat color and a top-coat color and hit-and-miss passes with a spackling knife that allow the base-coat color to show through

Color Wheel a circular device or tool with colors arranged in spectral order, beginning with red

Comb a tool, made of metal, rubber, plastic, or paper, used to create grain lines simulating wood textures

Complementary Colors colors directly across from each other on the color wheel

Contrasting Colors colors with strong intensities that are mostly used as accents; *see also* Complementary Colors

Cool Colors colors with a blue undertone; blue-green, blue, blue-purple, purple, red-purple, teal; some greens

Earth Colors yellow ochre, burnt umber, raw umber, burnt sienna, raw sienna, and black

Eclectic mixed styles and colors; most finishes work, depending on the predominant style

Eggshell a paint with a flat sheen; absorbs light, cleans up well, shows few flaws; *see also* Satin

Egg Tempera a traditional paint or coating made from an egg emulsion and pigment

English Country a traditional style favoring warm, slightly faded colors

Faux Finish a painted finish that simulates a texture such as marble, wood, or stone

Faux Wallpaper a faux-finishing technique that creates a pattern or repeated motif and that resembles wallpaper; a design on a wall made with a stencil, paper, paint, and glaze

Feathering a soft painted edge that is created when a brush is slowly lifted away from the surface while painting

Federal a traditional decorating and architectural style; *see* Regency or Federal

Flat a paint finish without luster; does not reflect light, cleans up poorly, hides flaws

Flogger a brush with long flexible horsehair bristles used for graining

Fluorescent Light usually light provided by a fluorescent tube that invigorates green, blue, and violet hues; washes out red, yellow, and orange; unflattering to yellow-undertone skin and colors

Formulas a prescription of ingredients used in fixed proportions

French Country a traditional style favoring light, pastel colors

Georgian a traditional style favoring scarlet red, emerald green with black and gold

Glaze a translucent overlay of a tinted or clear medium that's applied over a dry base coat; a few available glazes are alkyd, latex, oil, and acrylic

Gloss a paint finish or sheen that reflects light highly, cleans up well, shows every flaw

Gold Leaf very thin sheets of actual gold separated by tissue paper to protect it from breaking apart before use

Gouache water-soluble paint when wet or dry; mix with acrylic medium to make it indelible; brilliant colors and soft matte finish

Hue the gradation of a color; brightness, lightness, or saturation

Incandescent Light conventional tungsten lightbulb provides this light, which enhances yellow and orange, gives red a slightly orange tint; dulls blue and violet

Intensity the brightness of a color

Iridescent a term applied to a paint or glaze that is lustrous; also a colorful medium available in art-supply and specialty paint stores

Iridescent Strié a faux-finishing technique that uses an iridescent medium mixed into a glaze to achieve a shimmering, elegant effect

Japan Colors intense colors available in a limited range; dry to matte finish; available in some craft stores

Lacquer a clear or pigmented fast-drying coating; requires solvent for thinning and for cleaning paintbrushes and equipment

Latex Paint a water-based paint or coating that usually has a flat or semigloss finish; easy to apply and quick-drying

Level a device used for determining a horizontal plane; a bubble in a liquid reveals adjustment to the horizontal by movement of the bubble to the center of the glass tube

Marble metamorphic rock formed of calcite, dolomite, or dense limestone and other materials

Marbling a faux-finishing technique that suggests the coloring or markings of natural marble

Masking Tape used to cover a surface when painting an adjacent one; tack or stick quality of tape varies widely; if left on more than 24 hours can damage surface; available in 1/8- to 4-inch widths

Matte a finish that lacks luster or gloss; also a smooth, even surface free from highlights or shine

Metallic-Color Layering a faux-finishing technique of color layering that uses a metallic paint for the top coat, achieving an industrial or futuristic look

Mildew fungus growth, usually caused by too much moisture, lack of sunlight; remove with bleach before priming; use face mask and gloves to apply mildew-preventative paint

Modern a contemporary style favoring ultramarine, lilac, various reds with black and silver accents

Molding the trim or wood strip, used for decoration, around a door or window; also around a ceiling or floor; *see also* Wainscoting; Chair Rail; Baseboard

Monochromatic one color and a variation of the color

Mylar a thin and strong polyester film available at art-supply stores

Natural Light outside light; sunlight; or a combination of incandescent lightbulb and fluorescent tube; warms red, brightens blue, darkens green, may tone down yellow

Neoclassical a traditional style favoring reds, yellows, greens, and lilac

Neutral Colors white, off-white, browns, grays, black, charcoal, and sometimes metallic colors

Old World a traditional style or look of aged walls; created in a faux finish by applying paint or glaze in a hit-and-miss pattern and removing some of the paint or glaze

Oil-Based Glaze dries in 30 to 40 minutes; thicker than water-based glazes; can be thinned; tint only with Japan colors, artist's oils, or universal tints; requires paint thinner for cleanup

Oil-Based Paint a paint composed of resins that require solvent for reduction; paintbrushes and equipment must be cleaned in turpentine or thinner

Opaque a term applied to a paint or film that does not allow light to pass through

Overgrainer a tool for creating a wood-grain appearance in paint or glaze

Paint Fumes remember that many paint fumes and solvents are flammable; NO SMOKING; open windows to allow proper ventilation

Painter's Tape a paper tape lightly gummed on half its width; stiff, cannot be used on curves, doesn't stick to itself; best for short-term use; available in 2- to 6-inch widths

Paper Pressing a faux-finishing technique that uses pressing paper into wet paint or glaze and removing it to create a texture

Plumb Line a piece of cord or string with a weight attached; used to ensure straight vertical lines

Pigment a paint ingredient that provides color; helps coat and hide flaws in a painted surface

Polyurethane a synthetic, transparent seal used to protect wood or other surfaces

Predominant Color the color that stands out; the strongest color in a room

Primary Colors red, yellow, and blue

Primer a base-coat paint applied to wood or plaster to seal pores; a stable base for an undercoat of paint, applied before a top coat; varieties include alkyd or oil-based and latex or water-based paints

Ragging a faux-finishing technique using a cotton rag dipped in paint on a wall painted in a different color

Ragging Off a faux-finishing technique that involves first applying paint or glaze to a surface with a brush or roller, then using a cotton rag to remove paint or glaze

Rag Rolling a faux-finishing technique that involves using a rag like a rolling pin to apply paint to a surface

Rag Rolling Off a faux-finishing technique that combines rag rolling and sponging off sections of walls to remove a paint or glaze

Regency or Federal a traditional style favoring strong yellow, emerald with crimson, deep pinks and blues

Resin a synthetic or natural substance that's the main ingredient in paint that helps bind other ingredients together

Respirator a face mask that covers the mouth and nose and decreases exposure of the lungs to solvent fumes; masks range from simple paper to those with chemical filters

Roller Painting recommended on large surfaces; rolling is quicker and easier than brush work; leaves no brush marks; requires a *roller* (uses a cloth, flocking, or foam-covered head, a revolving cylinder that absorbs paint, held with a handle) and *roller tray* half-filled with paint; an extension pole attached to the roller handle allows the painter to reach high places

Rustic a faux-finishing technique applied to walls to make them appear to have the patina of age

Sanding Block a small block of wood with sandpaper attached that can fit in the hand and be used for sanding to maintain a flat surface

Sandpaper sheets of paper in coarse to fine grades used for abrading, or sanding a surface to make it smooth

Satin a paint finish or sheen between flat and gloss

Scandinavian Country a traditional style favoring cool, crisp colors with blue and white checks

Scraper a metal tool used to remove paint

Sealer a transparent liquid that seals and protects wood, wall, faux finishes, and painted surfaces

Secondary Colors orange, green, and violet

Semigloss a paint finish or sheen less reflective than gloss finish; cleans up very well, shows flaws

Sheen the finish of a paint, such as gloss, semigloss, eggshell, or flat

Shellac a medium or coating used to seal wood knots and to seal unpainted woodwork; available in clear, blond, and white; avoid using expired cans of shellac

Solvent a liquid used in paint and glaze that makes them more workable or smooth in application; evaporates when the paint or finish dries, allowing the paint to harden; also used for cleaning paintbrushes and equipment; *see also* Thinner

Spackle a compound for covering and hiding cracks and holes in plaster

Spackling Tape used to cover deep or persistent holes and cracks in walls; available at hardware stores; also called crack-repair screen

Spalter a shorthair or longhair brush for applying and smoothing oil glazes

Specialty Brushes used in decorative-painting techniques; varieties include spalter, stipple, flogger, overgrainer, stencil, and badger brushes

Sponging a faux-finishing technique using a sponge (natural or synthetic), dipped in paint and squeezed out, on a wall painted in a different color

Sponging Off a faux-finishing technique that involves applying paint or glaze to walls, then removing it with a sponge before it dries

Stain oil-based or water-based medium used for coloring wood; enhances the grain

Stencil a positive or negative design cutout made in cardboard, plastic, or another durable material used for repeating a pattern; paint, powder, ink, or another medium forced through the cutout recreates the design on another surface

Straining removing clumps and flakes from a can of paint by pouring it into a strainer made of pantyhose, cheesecloth, filter paper, or another material

Strié a French term for "striated" or scratched-glaze surface; glaze or paint is removed using a flogger, dragger, comb, or other tool(s)

Strié Waterfall a faux-finishing technique that varies a standard strié pattern and creates a waterfall appearance

Stippling an effect created by pressing the tips of a brush into a wet medium to produce a dotted (stippled) surface

Stippling Brush a hogs-hair brush used for stippling wet glazes, paints, and varnish; carefully clean and store so that bristles are not bent out of shape

Striping a decorative style with alternate thin bands or stripes, usually vertical, of two or more colors; as a faux finish may resemble wallpaper

Stripper a chemical used for removing paint from wood and metal surfaces; highly flammable

Tempera a traditional paint or coating with an albuminous or colloidal medium (such as an egg yolk) used as a vehicle instead of oil

Tertiary Colors colors created by mixing equal amounts of a primary and a secondary color

Thinner a volatile liquid, such as turpentine, used to thin paint; thinners for alkyd or oil-based paints are flammable; water-based paints use water as a thinner; *see also* Solvent

Tint a color that has white added

Tinting adding pigment or color to a glaze or paint

Tone a color that has both black and white added

Top Coat the last or finishing coat of paint on a surface

Translucent a term for a paint or film that allows some light to pass through

Transparent a term applied to a paint, film, or wash that allows light to pass through

Triad Harmony three colors that may be used as a color scheme; determined by placing a triangle on the color wheel so that the three corners point to three colors

Value the lightness to darkness of a color

Ventilation air flow in a room; allow fresh air to enter and circulate in a room when painting

Victorian a traditional style favoring deep, rich colors like deep blue, brown, olive green, and magenta

Wainscoting a protective or decorative finish wall covering applied to the lower part of an interior wall, often below a chair rail

Wallpaper a decorative paper applied to a wall with an adhesive

Warm Colors colors with yellow undertones; yellow, red-orange, yellow-orange, yellow-green, peach; also sometimes red, orange, mauve

Water-Based Glaze a thin glaze that dries in 20 minutes; difficult for working on large surfaces; can be tinted with latex paints, acrylic, casein, tempera, gouache, watercolor, and water-soluble pigments

Water-Based Paint a coating (paint), such as latex, that uses water as a solvent, dries quickly, cleans up quickly; can be removed with denatured alcohol when dry

Wash (Color) a thinned-down paint that allows a hint of the background color to show through

Wipe-On-Off Color a faux-finishing technique used on high-relief or carved molding to enhance the molding's details

Wood Knots darkened, circular spots naturally occurring in wood grain; sealed with primer, base coat, or shellac

metric equivalents

Capacity (Liquid & Dry Measures)

1 milliliter = 0.2 teaspoon = 0.07 tablespoon = 0.034 fluid ounce = 0.004 cup

1 teaspoon = 100 drops = 5 milliliters = $^1/_3$ tablespoon

1 tablespoon = 3 teaspoons = $^1/_2$ fluid ounce = 15 milliliters

1 fluid ounce = 2 tablespoons = 30 milliliters = 0.03 liter

1 gill = 4 fluid ounces = 7.22 cubic inches = 118.29 milliliters

1 cup = 16 tablespoons = 8 fluid ounces = 240 milliliters = 0.24 liter

1 pint = 2 cups = 480 milliliters = 0.47 liter

1 quart = 4 cups = 2 pints = 32 fluid ounces = 960 milliliters = 0.95 liter = 57.75 cubic inches

1 liter = 1,000 milliliters = 61.02 cubic inches = 34 fluid ounces = 4.2 cups = 2.1 pints = 1.06 quart (liquid) = 0.908 quart (dry) = 0.26 gallon

1 gallon = 4 quarts = 128 fluid ounces = 3.8 liters = 231 cubic inches

Weight (Avoirdupois)

1 gram = 0.035 ounce = 1,000 milligrams = 0.002 pound

1 ounce = 28 grams = 437.5 grains = 0.06 pound

100 grams = $3^1/_2$ ounces

1 pound = 16 ounces = 454 grams = 0.45 kilogram = 7,000 grains

1 kilogram = 2.2 pounds = 1,000 grams

Weight (Apothecaries')

1 dram = 3 scruples = 60 grains = 3.88 grams

1 ounce = 8 drams = 480 grains = 0.083 pound

1 pound = 12 ounces = 5760 grains = 0.37 kilogram

Distance

1 millimeter = 0.039 inch

1 inch = 25 millimeters = 2.54 centimeters = 0.025 meter

1 foot = 12 inches = 30 centimeters = 0.3 meter

1 yard = 3 feet = 36 inches = 90 centimeters = 0.9 meter

1 meter = 100 centimeters = 39.37 inches = 3.28 feet = 1.09 yards (1 yard + $3^2/_5$ inches) = 0.2 rods

Area

1 square centimeter = 0.15 square inch

1 square inch = 6.45 square centimeters

1 square foot = 0.09 square meter

1 square yard = 0.83 square meter

1 square meter = 10.76 square feet = 1.19 square yards

Volume

1 cubic centimeter = 1,000 cubic millimeters = 0.06 cubic inch

1 cubic inch = 16.38 cubic centimeters

1 cubic foot = 1728 cubic inches = 0.028 cubic meter = 0.037 cubic yard

1 cubic yard = 27 cubic meter = 0.76 cubic meter

1 cubic meter = 1,000,000 cubic centimeters = 35.31 cubic feet = 1.3 cubic yards

Temperature

To convert Centigrade (Celsius) to Fahrenheit degrees, use this formula:

$$9/5\ °C + 32 = °F$$

To convert Fahrenheit to Centigrade (Celsius) degrees, use this formula:

$$5/9\ (°F - 32) = °C$$

index